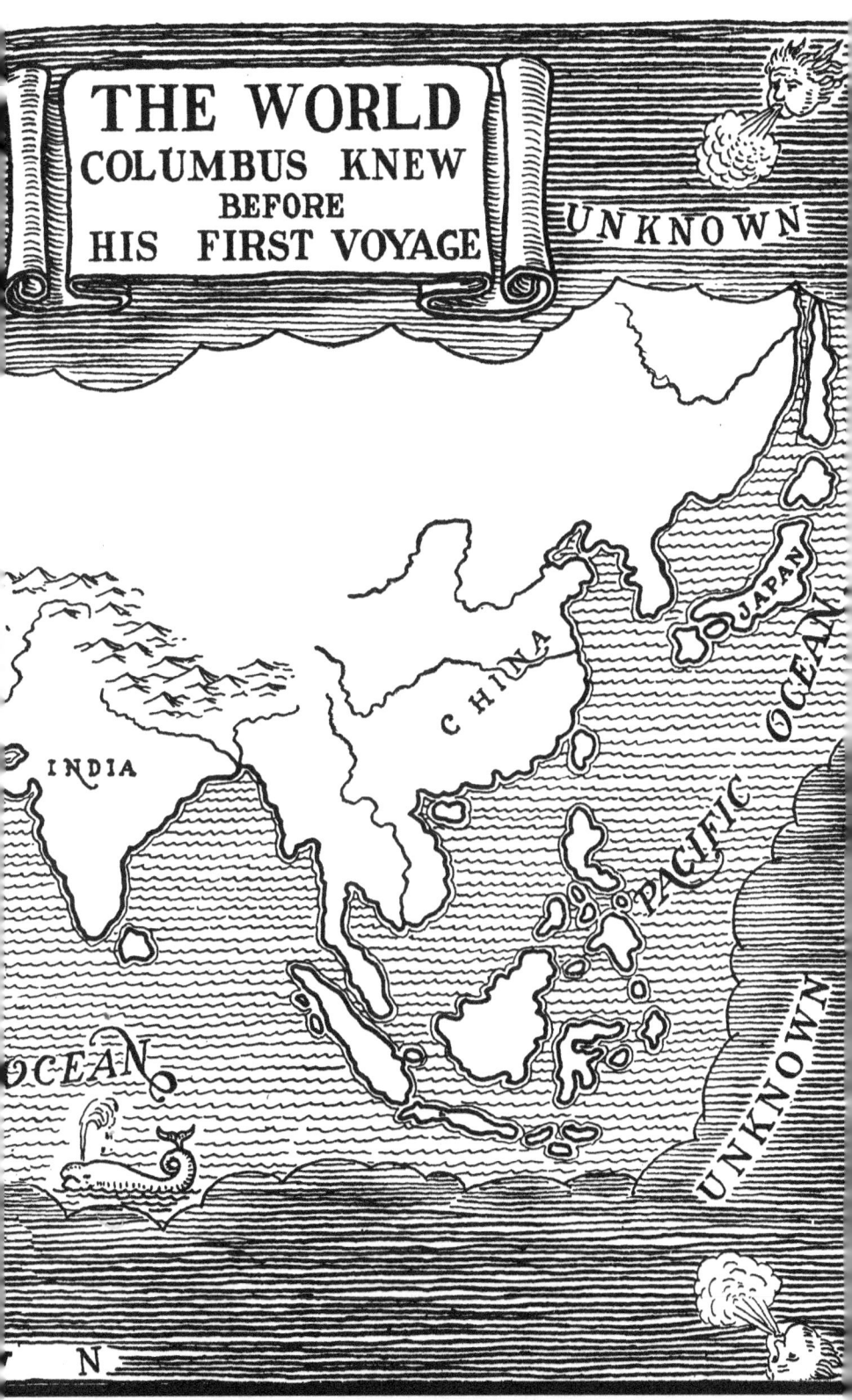

THOSE WHO DARED

THOSE WHO DARED

STORIES OF EARLY DAYS IN OUR COUNTRY

BY

CARRIE HUNTER WILLIS
AND
LUCY S. SAUNDERS

AUTHORS OF *Early Days in Virginia*
AND
The Story of Virginia
WITH ILLUSTRATIONS

CHAPEL HILL
THE UNIVERSITY OF NORTH CAROLINA PRESS

COPYRIGHT, 1935, BY
THE UNIVERSITY OF NORTH CAROLINA PRESS

THIS BOOK WAS DIGITALLY PRINTED.

TABLE OF CONTENTS

PART I
WESTWARD HO!

I.	COLUMBUS, THE BOY DREAMER	3
II.	PONCE DE LEÓN AND THE FOUNTAIN OF YOUTH	19
III.	WALTER RALEIGH, A FAVORITE KNIGHT	24
	THE LIBRARY; SELF-TESTING GAMES; SOMETHING TO DO	35, 36, 37

PART II
THE FIRST SETTLERS COME TO STAY

IV.	JAMESTOWN: CAPTAIN JOHN SMITH	41
V.	THE PILGRIMS	51
VI.	NEW YORK: HENRY HUDSON SAILS FROM THE WEEPERS' TOWER OF AMSTERDAM	60
VII.	PENN'S WOODS	73
VIII.	A FRIEND TO THE FRIENDLESS	83
	THE LIBRARY; SELF-TESTING GAMES; SOMETHING TO DO	89, 90, 91

PART III
CHILDREN OF LONG AGO

IX.	A LITTLE GIRL OF LONG AGO	95
X.	JACK AND PATSY CUSTIS AT MOUNT VERNON	100

Contents—*Continued*

XI. IN THE DAYS OF YOUNG JOHN QUINCY
ADAMS AND ABBY ADAMS . . . 109
THE LIBRARY; SELF-TESTING GAME;
SOMETHING TO DO 118, 119

PART IV

PIONEER LIFE IN THE DAYS OF DANIEL BOONE

XII. A BOY OF THE FRONTIER 123
XIII. DANIEL BOONE GOES TO WAR . . 127
XIV. THE BOONE'S PIONEER HOME . . 129
XV. HUNTING ADVENTURES 134
XVI. LIFE IN BOONESBORO 137
XVII. DANIEL BOONE GOES FARTHER WEST 142
THE LIBRARY; SELF-TESTING GAME;
SOMETHING TO DO 143, 144

PART V

THE COLONIES COME TOGETHER

XVIII. THE COLONISTS WANT TO BE FREE 147
XIX. THE SPIRIT OF THE PEOPLE . . . 154
XX. BENJAMIN FRANKLIN, OUR MESSENGER TO FRANCE 158
XXI. THE HERO OF THE NORTHWEST . . 164
XXII. FREEDOM IS WON WITH THE HELP OF FRIENDS FROM OVER THE SEA . . 172
XXIII. A PLAN TO LIVE BY: THE CONSTITUTION 176
THE LIBRARY; SELF-TESTING GAME;
SOMETHING TO DO 178, 179

Contents—*Continued*

PART VI
OUR COUNTRY—A NEW NATION

XXIV.	A LITTLE GIRL CROWNS A PRESIDENT	183
XXV.	BEGINNINGS OF A NEW NATION . .	187
XXVI.	A RIDE IN THE DAYS OF THE FIRST PRESIDENT	191
XXVII.	TWO VIRGINIANS OPEN THE DOOR TO THE WEST	195
XXVIII.	THE LAST OF THE PIRATES TURN PATRIOTS	206
	THE LIBRARY; SELF-TESTING GAME; SOMETHING TO DO . . 211, 212,	213

PART VII
PIONEERS! MORE PIONEERS!

XXIX.	PEOPLE GO WEST	217
XXX.	A FAMOUS GUIDE AND A PATHFINDER	221
XXXI.	THE FATHER OF TEXAS, STEPHEN F. AUSTIN	229
XXXII.	THE ALTAR OF TEXAS FREEDOM . .	233
	THE LIBRARY; SELF-TESTING GAME; SOMETHING TO DO 236,	237

PART VIII
SOMETHING NEW

XXXIII.	MAKING A MILL FROM MEMORY . .	241
XXXIV.	ELI WHITNEY INVENTS THE COTTON GIN	245
XXXV.	QUICK-SILVER BOB BUILDS A STEAMBOAT	250
XXXVI.	A FARMER BOY MAKES A REAPER .	254

Contents—*Continued*

XXXVII.	THE TOM THUMB RACES WITH A HORSE CAR	260
XXXVIII.	THE DOT AND DASH CODE CARRIES MESSAGES	264
XXXIX.	THE INDIA RUBBER MAN	269
	THE LIBRARY; SELF-TESTING GAME; SOMETHING TO DO	272, 273

PART IX
OUR COUNTRY REACHES FROM COAST TO COAST

XL.	THE OREGON TRAIL IS OPENED	277
XLI.	GOLD! GOLD! THE LAND OF GOLD!	283
XLII.	THE FORTY-NINERS AND HOW THEY TRAVELED	288
XLIII.	THE PONY EXPRESS	295
	THE LIBRARY; SELF-TESTING GAMES; SOMETHING TO DO	302, 303, 304

PART I
WESTWARD HO!

CHAPTER I

COLUMBUS, THE BOY DREAMER

How should you like to live in a city which has a dock and a harbor in the front yard and blue, blue water out beyond? Genoa, a city in Italy, has a dock and a harbor in the front yard and looks out across the blue water, but in the back yard a great mountain wall shuts the city off from her neighbors.

Long ago there lived in Genoa a weaver, named Domenico Columbus, and his wife. One day Domenico was called in from combing the tangled wool to see his first-born, a son.

"Now I have a son," he said proudly to his wife, "who will help me carry on this wool-combing business as I have done for my father."

But little Christopher, as the boy was called, did not like the ugly stiff comb which untangled the snarled wool. He did not like to run the wool through his fingers as his father did. In fact, Christopher did not like to smell the dusty wool—much less, to work with it.

Christopher wanted to play with make-believe ships. He would run away to the wharf. There he watched the strange vessels anchored in the harbor. He listened to the stories which the sailors told.

"When I am a man," Christopher said, "I am going to sea."

Those Who Dared

One day Christopher heard some men talking. These men were off the ships which had come from far-away India. They had brought spices, gums from trees, and silk to sell in Genoa. Columbus could smell the sweetness of the spices. The traders and merchants were arguing about the prices of their cargoes.

"I cannot pay so much for your silks and spices," said one merchant to a trader from India.

"But I cannot sell for less," answered the trader. "It took me months to go to India and return." At last the merchant bought the silks and spices and paid what the trader asked.

Christopher asked the trader about his trip to India and why it took him so long to go and come. "It is like this, my boy," the trader replied. "First I must have a strong vessel and a brave crew of sailors. Then I must sail with the winds. If they are kind and favorable I may reach India without delay. There I buy my silks, spices, and gums. These may have been brought on camels' backs from countries still farther east. Then I have to carry them over the long journey home again."

From then on Christopher was restless. He was eager to sail the far-off seas, to see the camels, to see the land where the natives lived who did the loading and unloading for the traders.

One day Christopher's father found him day-dreaming at the wharf, and he saw the eagerness in his son's eyes as he watched the ships drop anchor. Then he watched the boy's longing look as the ships sailed away. His

CHRISTOPHER COLUMBUS ON THE WHARF AT GENOA

father said, "If you cannot be happy as a wool-comber you may go to sea, but you must not stop school yet."

"I will study hard," Christopher promised. He studied reading, writing, and arithmetic, just as you do. He also studied Latin and drawing. Soon he was ready for the University. The study which Christopher liked best of all was that which taught him about the sea. This was called Navigation. He learned about the stars and about

Those Who Dared

the shore-lines of the world as people thought they were, in those days.

After he came home from the University, his father still hoped he would take up weaving. Christopher tried hard to please his father. He worked at combing the wool and weaving, but his heart was not in it. He was dreaming again of ships, of rolling seas, of capturing pirates.

Then, when he was just fourteen years old, his dreams began to come true. A kinsman who was a sailor agreed to let Christopher go with him on his trips.

Christopher now made many voyages. He sailed along the coast of Africa and of Europe. He also read about Marco Polo's travels in China and other countries of the East, and longed to go there himself.

THE WONDERFUL COUNTRY TO THE EAST

In the days before Columbus, Marco Polo with his father and his uncle returned from a long stay in China. They were dressed in very shabby clothes because they did not wish robbers to know that they carried with them great riches. In those days robbers were everywhere.

The Polos told the people of Venice, their home city, how great was the wealth of China and the other countries of the East. The people would not believe. The Polos then gave a party and invited their friends. After the feast, they brought in their old clothes and opened the seams. Out fell jewels and precious stones. They did this to show how great was the wealth of the East.

Columbus, the Boy Dreamer

As Columbus read of Marco Polo and the wonderful countries to the East, he made up his mind to try to reach the East by sailing west, around the world. Then he hoped to find this land where it was said that even the roofs of some of the houses were covered with gold.

To make such a voyage, Columbus needed money, men, and ships; and he did not have them. He was poor. He earned his living by making maps and charts. The future did not seem bright for him. The only way he could make this unknown voyage was by getting those who had money to believe in his plan.

THE DREAMER VISITS KINGS

Columbus was so sure the world was round that he wanted to show others that it was. He was sure, too, that he could make his dreams come true—that he could find a short route to India by sailing west.

Columbus had always believed in God. Now he believed that God had chosen him to find lands where Christ was not known. He wanted to take the faith of Christians to heathen lands. He never thought for one moment that he would fail.

Columbus determined to go to see King John of Portugal. He asked the King to give him ships and men to find the short route to India. If Columbus could do this, the King and Portugal would be very rich, and Columbus would be governor and share in the treasures, too.

The King listened very closely. Then he called in

COLUMBUS, WITH HIS LITTLE SON, EXPLAINING TO A FRIENDLY PRIEST HIS PLAN FOR FINDING THE EAST BY SAILING WEST

his wise men. After they heard Columbus' plans they were shocked.

"Columbus is crazy," the wise men told the King. "It is a dreamer's dream. We know that the earth is flat and that there are boiling seas beyond the dark green ocean. He cannot go east by sailing west!"

But the King was too much interested in Columbus' plans to give up. He talked it over with the Bishop.

"Let us keep Columbus waiting for a while," said the Bishop. "Get him to show you his charts and maps. Then send your own vessels over Columbus' route."

Columbus, the Boy Dreamer

This the King decided to do. His ships sailed as far as the outmost island. A storm came up and frightened the sailors. They returned to the King and said, "There is no truth in this dreamer's plan."

When Columbus found how he had been cheated, he was very angry, and started to another country to lay his plans before other rulers.

With his little son, he now went to Spain. When they reached there, a war was going on. King Ferdinand and Queen Isabella kept close to their army by moving their court from one place to another as the army changed its position. Columbus followed, hoping to see the rulers and tell them of his plans. But every time his hopes were high and he was sure he would soon see the King and Queen, news would come that the army was moving, and then the King's court would be moved, too. This went on for five or six years.

At last Columbus grew discouraged and felt that he must try his fortune elsewhere. With his son he started to leave Spain. One night he came to the home of a priest who was a learned man. Columbus told him of his hope of finding a shorter route to India by sailing west. The priest believed him. He said, "You must not leave Spain. I know Queen Isabella. I'll send a letter to her. I am sure she will see you then."

Columbus was delighted. At last someone thought he was right!

In those days letters were carried by hand. It took some time for the messenger to go to the court and bring

COLUMBUS BEFORE THE KING AND QUEEN OF SPAIN

a reply. When he returned, can you imagine the joy of Columbus?

The queen wished him to come at once to the Spanish court.

Columbus went without delay.

The queen heard his plans. She was so pleased that she said, "I will sell my jewels to furnish money, men, and ships for a voyage of such great promise."

Three vessels were fitted out—the "Santa Maria," the "Pinta," and the "Niña." It was very hard to find men to sail west on the unknown ocean. They did not

Columbus, the Boy Dreamer

know what would happen to them. Even the boldest seamen did not like to think of it. In August, when the ships sailed from Palos, gloom and sadness were cast over the whole place. The seamen were afraid. The families left behind said good-bye with tears. They feared that the ships and men would never return. The sails were set. The sailors raised the anchors. Slowly the ships moved out to sea. Columbus, the dreamer, was going to find his dreamland.

THE VOYAGE

At first the winds were favorable and the skies were clear. But after a time the ships struck great masses of seaweed. "Alas, alas!" complained the men. "We have come to the frozen ocean of which we were warned."

When they saw there was no ice, they complained because the winds had stopped blowing. There was a calm.

"We are going on a fool's errand," they told each other. "We shall not be able to find food or water. We are going farther and farther from the shores of Europe."

"Columbus is crazy," said a sailor. "Let us throw him into the ocean. We can then go home. We can say that he fell into the water when he was looking at the stars."

But no one had nerve to do this deed. Besides, the men had respect for Columbus, who was kind to them.

"Land, Land!" someone shouted. But the man had not seen land. It was only a low-hanging cloud. Weeks

"LAND! LAND!"

and weeks passed. A sailor picked up a thorn branch which had fresh thorns upon it. Another found a carved stick floating on the water. "Surely," declared the sailors, "we are near land." And all were cheered by the thought.

"A light! A light—a torch!" cried one of the men. All were so excited that night that they could not sleep. At two o'clock in the morning of October 12, 1492, land was sighted.

Columbus' dream had come true. He had reached land by sailing west. The shores of the New World lay before him. The "Santa Maria," "Pinta," and "Niña," which had sailed for days over strange seas, had reached port at last, and all the dangers of the long voyage were forgotten in the joy of the great discovery. Perhaps they

Columbus, the Boy Dreamer

had reached India, the land of rich silks and spices, of gold and precious stones. How glad Queen Isabella would be that she had faith in the strange plan of Columbus! What riches they could take back to the families they had left at home.

The New World

The island which now spread before Columbus was covered with trees. The naked natives, filled with wonder, came from the woods and gathered on the shores. They gazed with awe at these men who seemed to come from the skies on their ships with sails like the wings of birds.

Columbus went ashore. Richly dressed in scarlet, surrounded by his men, he carried the royal banner of Spain and one of his captains carried a banner of the Green Cross, Columbus' own flag. On landing, he knelt, threw himself on the earth, kissed the ground, and with tears of joy thanked God. The men did the same. Columbus then rose, drew his sword, and in the name of King Ferdinand and Queen Isabella took possession of the island.

All were most joyous. The men crowded about Columbus. Some threw their arms around him. Some kissed his hands. Those who had given him greatest trouble on the voyage cast themselves at his feet and begged to be forgiven. Always kind and gentle, Columbus was glad to forget the past and to look forward to the good things which this new country had to give.

COLUMBUS DISCOVERS THE NEW WORLD

He named the island on which they landed San Salvador, which means "Holy Savior." He called the people "Indians," because he thought they were near the coast of India.

As Columbus visited other islands, he claimed them, too, for Spain. From the beauty and richness of this new land, he was sure that it must be the country in the East of which Marco Polo had written. But we know now

AND CLAIMS IT FOR THE KING AND QUEEN OF SPAIN

that he had not found a new way to China or India. He had discovered a New World.

On the night of Christmas Eve Columbus' ship was wrecked while it was sailing off the coast of one of the islands. At first this seemed a great hardship, but the natives brought gold for trade. They gave large pieces of gold for very small things which the Spaniards had. A gold coronet, gold plates, and other presents were

Those Who Dared

made to Columbus, and he was told that much more could be found in other parts of the island. The disappointment which the Spaniards had felt at not finding gold now turned to hope.

They built a fortress from the wreck of the ship. Here were left thirty-nine men who would search for gold.

Early in January, Columbus said good-bye and, with the other members of his party, sailed away on the voyage home.

Columbus Returns

They had a stormy trip. At times it seemed as if their ships would certainly be lost at sea. In the midst of these perils, Columbus thought of a way to save the story of his discoveries if the ships should sink. He wrote a short account of his voyage and of the newly-found islands. This he sealed and directed to the King and Queen of Spain. He then wrapped it in a waxed cloth, which was placed in the center of a cake of wax. The whole he put into a barrel and threw into the sea.

At last they rode out the storms and reached Europe on March 4. When Columbus' ship was seen at Palos on March 15, bells were rung, shops were closed, and people thronged to meet their returned friends and bold adventurers.

Columbus wrote King Ferdinand and Queen Isabella of his arrival. They replied, telling of their delight and ordering Columbus to come at once to court.

He started immediately, taking with him six Indians,

Columbus, the Boy Dreamer

and the gold, the cotton and other things he had brought from the New World.

A great reception was given in Barcelona, where the King and Queen received him. The parade was led by the Indians painted in their savage style. After them came men carrying live parrots and stuffed birds brought from the new land. Great care was taken to show the gold coronet and bracelets, so that everyone could see the wealth of the new islands. Then came Columbus on horseback surrounded by a company of men in shining armor, with bright-colored banners. The streets, the windows, and even the roofs of houses were filled with people anxious to get sight of the hero.

The rulers had ordered their throne placed in the public square, under a covering of gold. Here, when Columbus came near, they arose to greet him as only those of highest rank were received.

When Columbus told them of the wonderful new country that he had discovered, the King and Queen sank on their knees and with tears of joy thanked God for His goodness.

It would have been better for Columbus, if his ventures had ended here. But he made three other voyages to the New World. Men became jealous of him. Enemies arose. Once, he was returned home in chains. When Queen Isabella saw him, she wept, but she did not live to see his wrongs made right. He died a broken-hearted man, never knowing the great discovery he had made.

Those Who Dared

Today in the harbor of Genoa, over which Columbus, the boy dreamer, looked, one may see many ships bringing in their cargoes from the ports of that New World which he found by sailing westward across the unknown ocean—the great land which is the gift of Christopher Columbus to the world.

CHAPTER II

PONCE DE LEÓN AND THE FOUNTAIN OF YOUTH

Other daring men followed Columbus into the New World. Many came in search of gold. Others settled and made homes. Among those who came over was a man named Ponce de León, who conquered the island of Porto Rico and became its governor. This prince was wealthy, brave, and noble, but he was no longer young.

The Indians told Ponce de León of a wonderful fountain whose waters made old people young.

Ponce de León longed to find this fountain and to learn more of the beautiful country of the New World. With a company of men and ships he sailed from Porto Rico to find "the fountain of youth." On Easter Sunday he came to a "lovely land of flowers" which he called Florida.

Ponce de León did not become young again, but if you go to Florida today and visit the quaint old town of St. Augustine, you will find there among the cedars, oaks, and magnolias a fountain called, "The Fountain of Youth." Near this you will see a cross of stone laid in the ground. The body of the cross is made of fifteen stones, and the arms of thirteen stones. This shows the date, 1513, the year Ponce de León discovered Florida.

PONCE DE LEÓN CLAIMS FLORIDA FOR GOD AND THE KING OF SPAIN

It is said that he planted this cross and took possession of the new land in the name of the King of Spain. We do not know that the planting of the cross was his work, but we do know that he claimed this land for his country.

Ponce de León returned to Spain and told the King of the beautiful country he had found. He asked the King to let him settle the land. The King gave his consent and in a few years Ponce de León came back to the coast of Florida.

By this time many of the Indians in Florida had been

Ponce de León

taken as slaves. This changed the friendly natives to warlike enemies. When they saw Ponce de León and his men begin building houses, the Indians attacked the white men fiercely. Ponce de León was wounded and returned to Cuba. There soon afterwards he died, but the lovely land he had discovered attracted others to her shores.

THE OLDEST TOWN IN OUR COUNTRY

Years later the King sent other men to plant the Spanish colony which Ponce de León had planned. This time the leader was prepared for the Indians. He came with troops, guns, and stores. Sailing along the coast of Florida, he reached a little inlet of water. There the Spaniards seized the dwelling of an Indian chief. A very strange dwelling it was. The walls were built of whole tree trunks. Around this, to make it stronger and safer, the Spaniards threw up banks of sand. They named this place St. Augustine, because it was founded on St. Augustine's Day. This was in 1565, and was the beginning of the oldest town now in our country.

The people of St. Augustine fought not only the Indians, but also their white neighbors the French and later the English. Even today, the quiet little city shows marks of these conflicts of long ago.

Not far from the Fountain of Youth stands Fort Marion, which was called San Marco in the early days. The building of the fort, like a castle of olden times, took more than one hundred years. Some of its walls are forty feet thick. These walls and the watch-towers still stand.

THE CASTLE OF SAN MARCO (NOW FORT MARION) IN ST. AUGUSTINE, BUILT BY THE SPANIARDS, 1637-1756

Some of the old guns have been left mounted on the walls, but you may now enter the fort without fear. Even in the secret dungeons there is no longer any danger. Grass is now growing in the moat, the deep wide ditch around the walls, which in olden days was filled with water to keep enemies from crossing.

Today as you follow the guide through the fort and hear the stories of the past, you will see in your mind clear pictures of the brave men who lived in other days.

The story is told that once two Indians were impris-

Ponce de León

oned in a room of the fort. In this room was one small window, with iron bars across it. The Indians thought, "If we starve ourselves we may get thin enough to slip between those bars." So they ate very little. When they had lost a great deal of weight, they slipped through the bars, jumped into the water below, and swam away to freedom.

An old Indian chief was a prisoner also, but he would make no effort to escape. He said, "The white man put me in here and the white man must take me out." The white man did take him out, but he died only a short time afterwards.

The Spaniards did not trust only to their fort for safety, but, like many cities in the Old World, they built a wall around their town. The entrance to the old St. Augustine was by a draw-bridge through the city gate. Today the pillars of the gate are still standing, but the gate itself and the draw-bridge have gone, like the enemies of the old city.

Old houses and narrow streets remind one of the city of long ago. The new city remembers the man who discovered the "land of flowers." A wealthy citizen, Dr. Anderson, gave to the city a monument in memory of Ponce de León, of whom it was said that he was "mightier in deed than in name."

CHAPTER III

WALTER RALEIGH, A FAVORITE KNIGHT

The sea! Gold! A new world! These were magic words in the days when Walter Raleigh was born in Devon, near the town of Plymouth, on the southern coast of England. In Plymouth lived men who had sailed the sea. There sailors came and told stories of adventure. They told of the newly found country beyond the sea. They told of the strange people who lived there. They told of the wealth of the country, with its mines of silver and gold; and they told how shiploads of these riches were being taken to Spain.

As Raleigh grew older, he loved to listen to the stories of the sailors. He dreamed of a day when he too would sail the sea. He would go up to London to see the Queen, just as his older half-brother, Humphrey Gilbert, had done. Perhaps she would help him plant an English colony in the New World. They would all grow rich. England would get some of that vast treasure of gold and silver which was now going to Spain. But Raleigh's family put an end to his dreams by sending him off to college.

While he was at college, he heard that the Huguenots, a people in France, were being cruelly treated because they did not worship like others.

"I am going to France," Raleigh said to his friends. "I

SIR WALTER RALEIGH, "A KNIGHT OF THE OCEAN-SEA"

Those Who Dared

am going to fight for the Huguenots." And off he went to France and became a soldier. Some years later, when news came that the Irish were in revolt against England, Raleigh headed a company of men and did some good fighting in Ireland.

When he returned to England he met Queen Elizabeth. That royal lady was dressed as a queen should be—in silks, satins, and laces. Of course her slippers were as dainty as her lovely clothes. There is a famous story told about Raleigh and the Queen. Raleigh saw her pause when she came to a muddy spot. He sprang forward, pulled his red velvet cloak from his shoulders, and spread this over the muddy spot. The Queen stepped upon it and her pretty slippers were not soiled. Whether the story is true or not, Queen Elizabeth was pleased with the gallant soldier. She sent for him to come to the court.

Raleigh was excited. Now he could tell the Queen his dreams of planting a colony in the New World. He dressed himself in his finest clothes. Raleigh was very tall and handsome. He was full of fun and had a ready answer for everything said to him. The Queen was more pleased with him than ever, and he soon became one of the favorites at her court.

Walter Raleigh now told Queen Elizabeth how eager he was to plant a colony of English people in the New World. She listened attentively. Then she said, "You have my royal permission." Raleigh expected to go to America himself, but the Queen would not agree to this.

SIR WALTER RALEIGH SAID OF QUEEN ELIZABETH, "WE, HER TRUE AND OBEDIENT VASSALS, SHALL ALWAYS LOVE HER, SERVE HER, AND OBEY HER TO THE END OF OUR LIVES"

"I will help you outfit your expedition," she said, "but you cannot go. You are the captain of my guards." Raleigh was disappointed, but he knew he must obey the Queen. He hastened to make ready for the expedition. He bought the strongest boats he could find. He asked only those men to go who, he thought, would be brave and true. When all was ready he said to the two captains, "Sail and explore the coast north of Florida. Try

Those Who Dared

to keep away from the Spanish settlements southward."

Time passed slowly for Walter Raleigh while his expedition was gone. Though he enjoyed the gay life of the court, he was anxious to know what his men were doing.

At last news came that the ships had returned. How pleased Raleigh was with the reports which they brought of "the fair and luxuriant lands" across the sea! How interested he was in the two Indians, Manteo and Wanchese, whom the captains brought to England!

Roanoke Island

Queen Elizabeth now helped Raleigh with another expedition. The next year they sent a company of men to Virginia. Raleigh's cousin, Sir Richard Grenville, was the commander of the ships that brought the colonists over. Ralph Lane was governor, and John White was the artist who painted the first pictures of the natives in the country. These men settled on what is now Roanoke Island in North Carolina.

But they did not make any gardens or build strong houses. They began to hunt for gold. They wanted to get rich and return to England.

At first some of the Indians were friendly. Manteo liked the "Pale Faces," as the Indians called the English. He showed the men how to hunt and fish. He showed some of them how to plant the maize, which we call corn. But many of the Indians were very angry at the English, and this is how it came about. Before Sir Rich-

Sir Walter Raleigh

ard Grenville sailed back to England, he spent some time exploring the country. One day he missed a silver cup. He thought the Indians had stolen it, and he decided to punish all the Indians. He commanded his men to burn the Indian villages and the patches of corn. The English did wrong in this. The Indians thought it was wicked to burn food. They were very angry with the Pale Faces, and from that time the Indians became enemies to the English.

All this made matters worse, for in the meantime the English found no gold. The men were homesick. They had left their wives and mothers in far-away England. They did not like to cook and mend. They became very unhappy.

When Sir Francis Drake came to the island on his way to England, the men begged Governor Lane to let them go, too. Governor Lane knew that his men were not able to make a home for themselves in a strange country, and so he consented.

What a great disappointment it was to Raleigh when his colony returned! But he was more than ever determined to try again. He went at once to see the Queen and ask her to help.

The Lost Colony

"Your Majesty," begged Raleigh, "Let us try again to plant our colony in Virginia. This time we will send the wives of the men. Then they will not become homesick or dissatisfied."

Those Who Dared

Once more the Queen agreed. Raleigh bought ships and chose men whose wives were willing to share the dangers with them. John White, who had been the artist for the other colony, was asked to be governor.

Governor White and his colony landed on Roanoke Island in the summer. The people were delighted when they saw the lovely flowers blooming everywhere and heard the sweet songs of the birds. They found some herbs which they picked, and the women cooked them in the pots they had brought from England.

Some men cut down trees, and others began building rough houses. The women helped spade up the ground, and soon they had garden plots ready for seeds.

Governor White had brought with him his own daughter and her husband, Ananias Dare. They built a cabin, too. One day in August the whole village was thrown into great excitement. "What is it?" the men asked as they returned from the day's work.

The Dare's have a new baby," the women told them. "And the Governor is as pleased over it as the young parents are."

"What shall you name her?" someone asked Mrs. Dare.

"Why, we shall call her Virginia, for this lovely land to which she has come," replied Mrs. Dare. So far as is known, little Virginia Dare was the first English baby born in this country.

Before the baby was two weeks old, her grandfather, Governor White, returned to England. His colony needed more supplies of all kinds, even food.

ALL THAT WAS LEFT OF THE "LOST COLONY"

"I will come again soon," the Governor told his people, "but in case I am delayed and you should be forced to leave here, carve the name of the place to which you go on a tree or a post here in the village, and if you are in great trouble when you go, carve a cross above it."

Then Governor White sailed away. In England, he found his country at war with Spain. He had to wait four years before he could get his supplies.

He was very anxious about his colony. When he finally started back to Virginia, he urged the sailors to speed the boat as fast as they could. At last he reached Roanoke Island. It was too dark to land that night, but they saw a big campfire in the woods. The Englishmen

Those Who Dared

sounded a trumpet call, and sang many English songs to show who they were. But the next morning when they landed, the island seemed to be deserted. Then they found the letters "C. R. O." carved on a tree, but there was no cross above it. When Governor White reached the place where the settlers had lived, how his heart ached to find it deserted! Even the houses were stripped and torn down, but a high fence of the trunks of large trees had been built around the village. Governor White and his men searched for another sign to tell them where the colonists had gone. At last they noticed a tree or post at the right side of the gate. The bark had been stripped off in a place about five feet up, and the word, "CROATOAN" was carved there, but again there was no cross to show that the colonists had been in distress when they left. Governor White was now glad, because Croatoan was the place where Manteo was born, and the Indians there were friendly. He planned to go there to hunt for the colonists, but bad storms made it impossible, and so he sailed back to England. Nothing was ever heard of the Lost Colony.

This made the heart of Raleigh very sad. He was in great trouble now, too, because he had lost favor with Queen Elizabeth. He was no longer one of her favorites, and before he could win his place back, the Queen died.

The New King Unfriendly to Raleigh

The new ruler of England, after Queen Elizabeth's death, was James I. He heard that Raleigh was working

SIR WALTER RALEIGH IN PRISON, WRITING HIS "HISTORY OF THE WORLD"

Those Who Dared

against him, and so he had Raleigh thrown into the Tower of London—an old fort used as a prison. There was a trial, and then the order was given to behead Sir Walter. The fateful day came. The brave knight was ready for death. Then the King ordered him to be sent back to prison. Many people remembered the gay courtier. They went to visit him in the Tower and found him as charming as ever, even though he was a prisoner.

Twelve years passed. During this time Raleigh wrote a part of his *History of the World*. He did not live to finish this book. If you should go to London today you could see the room in which he spent his last years. You could see the walls of the great Tower of London, on which he walked as he thought and planned. He still dreamed, too, of other expeditions. Almost within sight of the Tower, ships were fitted out, which later landed at Jamestown.

He finally persuaded his friends to ask the King to let him sail for South America where he was sure he could find gold. Permission was granted by the King, and off Sir Walter sailed. But fortune had indeed forsaken him. He returned to England in disgrace because he had failed. Once more he was thrown into prison. The King had the old death sentence brought forth again. This was done so quickly that this time there were no friends to plead for Raleigh.

The gallant knight was still witty, courteous, and brave. On his way to the scaffold in the chill damp of the early morning he passed an old man without a hat.

Westward Ho!

Quickly Raleigh grasped his own cap and threw it to the man saying, "Take this! You have greater need of it than I!"

The King had Raleigh killed, but the English colonies of which the brave knight dreamed continued to grow. He may rightly be called the father of the first English colonies in the New World.

THE LIBRARY
Stories in Other Books

"The Story of Columbus," "The Story of Ponce de León," "Sir Walter Raleigh Tried to Get America for England," in *Our Nation Begins*, by Eugene C. Barker, William E. Dodd, and Walter P. Webb.

"Spices And a New World," in *These United States and How They Came to Be*, by Gertrude Hartman.

"A Weaver's Son Finds a New World," "The Land of Humpbacked Cows," in *How the Old World Found the New*, by Eunice Fuller Barnard and Lida Lee Tall.

"Columbus' First Voyage," in *Real Stories of the Geography Makers*, by John Thomson Faris.

"Columbus and The Egg," "The Fountain of Youth," in *Thirty More Famous Stories*, by James Baldwin.

"The Early Years of Columbus, The First Voyage of Columbus, Later Voyages of Columbus," "The Quest for a Fountain," "Sir Walter Raleigh, Pioneer," in *Founders of Our Country*, by Fanny E. Coe.

"The Fountain of Youth," in *The Voyager*, by Padriac Colum.

"A Great Adventure," in *The Story of Virginia*, by Carrie Hunter Willis and Lucy S. Saunders.

"The Red Velvet Cloak," "Baby Virginia," in *History Stories for Primary Grades*, by John Walter Wayland.

Those Who Dared

"When Columbus Discovered America," "Virginia Dare," in *American History Stories for Very Young Readers*, by Eva March Tappan.

SELF-TESTING GAMES

Game I

This is a choosing game. Choose the right word. Write in a column the numbers 1 to 10. After each number, place the word or words which make true the sentence having the same number. Each correct answer counts 2.

1. Columbus was born in the city of (Venice, Genoa).
2. He liked to play (with make-believe ships, with his father's tools).
3. Marco Polo told about the wealth of (China and the East, America and the West).
4. Columbus thought he could reach the East (by sailing through the Arctic Ocean, by sailing west).
5. He placed his plans before (the King of Portugal, the King of England).
6. He finally secured help from (the King of Italy, the King and Queen of Spain).
7. Men (wished to go, dreaded to go) with Columbus on this unknown voyage.
8. Three ships left Palos, a seaport in Spain, in August. They reached an island across the ocean on October 12 (1607, 1492).
9. Columbus and his men visited other islands. One of their ships was (burned, wrecked).
10. When they returned to Spain, they were (received with great honor, not noticed).

The highest possible score is 20. What is your score?

Westward Ho!
Game II

This is a matching game. On a sheet of paper copy the words in Column I. Then write the word in Column II opposite the one in Column I to which it belongs. There are ten points. Each point counts 2.

I	II
Ponce de León	friendly Indian
Sir Walter Raleigh	land of flowers
St. Augustine	Queen of England
Lost Colony	name of new country
Elizabeth	a favorite knight
Virginia Dare	a Spanish fort
Florida	oldest town
Manteo	first English baby in America
Virginia	Fountain of Youth
San Marco	Roanoke Island

The highest number of points is 20. How many points did you make?

Choose Something to Do

1. Act or pantomime the following scenes in the life of Columbus. Posters may be made announcing what the scenes will be.

   a. Columbus Watching the Merchants and Traders at the Wharf.
   b. Columbus and His Father at the Wharf.
   c. The Polos' Feast.
   d. Columbus before the King of Portugal.
   e. Columbus and His Son at the Home of the Priest.
   f. Columbus before the King and Queen of Spain.
   g. Columbus Claiming the New Land for Spain.
   h. On His Return to Spain, Columbus before the King and Queen.

2. Write a letter such as Columbus might have written to the Spanish rulers and placed in the barrel.

Those Who Dared

3. After looking at the map in the front of this book, make a map of the world as people thought it was before Columbus discovered America. Choose your own way of making it.
4. Make a cross showing the date Ponce de León reached the so-called "Fountain of Youth." See the picture on p. 20.
5. Build a fort like San Marco.
6. Draw scenes showing:
   a. Raleigh Meeting Queen Elizabeth
   b. Manteo and Wanchese on Board the Ship for England
   c. Governor White Leaving for England
   d. Governor White's Return to Roanoke Island.

PART II
THE FIRST SETTLERS COME TO STAY

CHAPTER IV

JAMESTOWN: CAPTAIN JOHN SMITH

Sir Walter Raleigh had lost so much money that he had to give up all his claims to land in Virginia, but other important Englishmen were interested in the New World; so they formed two companies, which they called the London Company and the Plymouth Company, to carry on the work of settlement. They asked King James to give them land in Virginia and to let them send over a colony to settle.

The King granted their request and the first colony was sent out by the London Company.

Now King James did a very strange and foolish thing. He did not tell the colonists which men were to be in charge of the colony, but he gave a list of their names to Captain Newport. This list was locked in a strong box.

"I bid you God speed," the King said, "and I charge you not to open this box until you reach Virginia."

Captain Newport was in command of the flag ship, the "Sarah Constant," which was followed by two other ships, the "Godspeed," and the "Discovery." Captain Gosnold, who had been to Virginia before, was in charge of the "Godspeed." What a mistake that Gosnold was not in command of the expedition! He knew more about the Virginia coast than any of the others.

From the beginning, the voyage was stormy both on

Those Who Dared

the sea and on the ships. The gentlemen settlers began to dispute. The sailors began to quarrel.

Men turned to John Smith for advice. Then they asked each other, "Who is this John Smith?"

First one and then another told something of Smith's adventures. One said that John Smith had run away from home when a young boy and had become a sailor. He had traveled all over France and most of Europe. Once he had sailed with a band of religious pilgrims. A terrible storm swept over them. The pilgrims said, "There is a wrong-doer on this ship. Let us cast lots to find out the one who is not a true believer; then we will throw him overboard." John Smith had to tell the pilgrims that he did not believe as they did. When they heard this, they threw him into the raging sea. They thought that if they did this, they would not be shipwrecked.

The brave young sailor, John Smith, was even then a good swimmer. He kept afloat and was saved by swimming until he reached shore.

Three Turks' Heads Upon a Shield

Smith longed to be a soldier, too. He went off to fight in Europe. There he met Turks who were fighting the people of Austria.

Smith got into a dispute with some Turks.

"Prove what you say!" shouted the Turks. "Will you fight against one of our brave men and thus settle who is right?"

Captain John Smith

"Aye! Aye!" agreed John Smith. So they sent a Turk to fight a duel with Smith. They fought with spears, and John Smith killed the Turk by piercing him with a spear.

"Will you fight another Turk?" asked the men.

"Aye! Aye!" agreed Smith, who could use a pistol as well as a spear.

So the second Turk was shot.

"You have been playing in luck," declared the men. "Prove yourself the third time."

Now John Smith was a fine swordsman and he fought and killed the third Turk with a sword.

Some people doubt the story of Smith's fight with the Turks, but we know that when he was made a knight, on his shield were engraved three Turks' heads.

SMITH A PRISONER

After hearing all these stories about Captain John Smith, the sailors for a time were more friendly with him. But as the days passed and they began to doubt if they would ever see land, troubles returned. They grew jealous of Smith, and did not trust him. Even his best friends turned against him. They accused him of planning to kill the captains and put himself in command. Finally Captain Newport had him put in chains as a prisoner.

At last the cry of "Land! Land!" settled for a time their quarrels and disputes. The voyage was about to end.

Those Who Dared

A storm drove the boats past two points of land called capes. The colonists named one Cape Charles and the other Cape Henry in honor of the two sons of King James. They anchored at Cape Henry on Sunday, April 26.

Some of the men were eager to go on land and see the new country. They found ripe strawberries, climbed sand dunes, and saw Indians. These savages did not welcome the new-comers, as the Indians had done on Roanoke Island. They followed the whites to their boats and wounded two of their number.

On board the ship at Cape Henry, the colonists opened the sealed box, and read the seven names of those on the list for the Council, which was to govern the colony. Gosnold's name was first and Smith's second.

The colonists decided not to stay at Cape Henry. The land was sandy with only scrubby trees. The Indians were unfriendly. Then, too, they wanted to be farther away from the coast because they feared the Spaniards might fall upon them. So the English sailed up a broad river which they called the James River in honor of their king.

After some time, they came to a long strip of land. They liked the tall strong trees here, which would make good timber for their houses. They felt, too, that on this strip of land they could more easily protect themselves from the Indians. So on May 13, 1607, they anchored and called the place Jamestown. Before they went on shore the Council chose Wingfield president.

Captain John Smith
SMITH'S TRIAL

Now when the president and his Council met, Captain Smith should have had a place with them. But Wingfield, like Newport, was opposed to Smith.

"You cannot sit in the Council," Smith was told.

"Let us send him back to England for trial," said some.

"I have done no wrong, for which I should be sent back to England," said Smith. "I refuse to go. I demand a trial here."

"That is only fair," others agreed.

A trial was given.

"What have you against this man?" asked Wingfield.

"There is nought I can say against him," answered first one and then the others. "He tried only to do the right thing. He did what he thought was best for us."

"You have accused Captain Smith unjustly," declared some members of the colony. "You must pay him damages." So they paid Captain Smith two hundred pounds in English money.

And what do you think he did with this money? He put it into the treasury for the good of all the colony.

Now a good preacher named Robert Hunt had come over with the settlers. He asked God's blessing on the colony when they started their new home at Jamestown. He liked Captain Smith. He had seen that Smith was a leader of men. The next Sunday after Captain Smith had taken his seat in the Council, the heart of the good preacher was filled with joy that justice had been done and that peace had come to the little colony.

CAPTAIN JOHN SMITH TRADES BEADS FOR CORN TO KEEP THE COLONISTS FROM STARVING

Captain Smith and the Indians

Captain Smith saw that food for the colonists would not last until they could get more from England. He was not afraid of the Indians. With a few men, he went down the James River to trade with them for corn. The savages would not listen to the whites until after Captain Smith had captured their idol, Okee, which the Indians had made of skins, stuffed with moss, to be one of their gods. To get Okee again in their hands the Indians were quite willing to give their corn to Captain Smith.

With blue beads and other trinkets, which he gave to the Indians, Smith would get bushels of corn for the colonists. By his cleverness and courage he kept the Jamestown colony from starving.

Captain John Smith

But Smith was interested not only in getting food for the colonists, but in finding out about the country. He made trips to explore the Chesapeake Bay and the rivers running into it. Once he went up the Chickahominy River. When the stream grew too small for his larger boats, he took two of his men and some Indians in a smaller boat farther up the stream. With an Indian as guide, he left the men in the boat and went out to explore the country. Soon he heard a noise which made him fear his men were in trouble. He looked up and saw Indians standing near him. Other Indians came from behind trees. Quickly Smith seized the Indian guide and placed him in front of himself as a shield. With his eyes on the Indians, he tried to withdraw from them, but stepped into a muddy swamp. He could go no farther. The Indians gathered around him. Captain Smith was a prisoner. The savages said his men in the boat had been killed. Smith showed no fear. He let them see his compass with its needle pointing north. The Indians thought that this worked by some magic power. They took their prized prisoner from village to village for others to see. Even the children gathered around him. For them, he made baskets of chestnut hulls and monkeys of hickory nuts.

Smith was then taken before the great King Powhatan. Here he was treated with the greatest courtesy. They brought him water and a towel of turkey feathers. A feast of turkey and deer was served.

After this the Indians held a council of war and de-

POCAHONTAS, THE INDIAN PRINCESS, SAVED CAPTAIN JOHN SMITH'S LIFE, WAS BAPTIZED AS THE "LADY REBECCA," MARRIED JOHN ROLFE, WAS PRESENTED AT THE ENGLISH COURT, AND DIED AND WAS BURIED IN ENGLAND

cided that Smith should die. Stones were placed on which he should lay his head. Over him stood a huge Indian warrior ready to crush out the brains of the captive. All was ready for the blow to fall, when Pocahontas, a little Indian maid, rushed forward, threw herself on Captain Smith, and begged her father, King Powhatan, to spare the life of this brave prisoner.

Perhaps Powhatan was glad to save the life of this man who seemed to know no fear. At any rate, the request

Captain John Smith

of his daughter was granted, and in a few days Smith returned to Jamestown. He carried with him the friendship of the little Princess Pocahontas, who was always loyal to the whites. Smith tells us this story in his book on Virginia. Some people doubt that it really happened, but we know that Pocahontas was a friend to the English and that she is one of the most lovable characters in our history.

Later when Smith became president of the Council, he had houses built and the fort made stronger. Everyone was made to work. The lazy gentlemen did not enjoy Smith as a leader. He himself continued to trade with the Indians for food.

One day Captain Smith went up the James River to settle a dispute with the Indians. A bag of powder exploded in the boat. Smith was badly burned. The pain was so great that he jumped into the river. There were no good doctors at Jamestown. The burns refused to heal; so he had to return to England for treatment.

Captain Smith did not return to Jamestown again, but later he went to the northern part of Virginia and explored that country. He made maps of this section, which he named New England. For this work, he was given the title "Admiral of New England."

Smith had many enemies, but the men who knew him best loved him. They said that John Smith never asked them to go into any danger which he was not willing to share. They said, too, that John Smith disliked laziness, falsehood, and foolish pride. He was strictly honest in

Those Who Dared

all his dealings, not only with his own people but with the Indians. He liked what men did, rather than what they said.

Jamestown is the oldest English settlement in the New World. That the little colony lived through those first trying years is due more to Captain John Smith than to any other one person.

This is what his friends had carved upon his tombstone in London, "Here lies one conquered that has conquered Kings."

CHAPTER V

THE PILGRIMS

"We are going on a long journey. We really are pilgrims," said the men and women who had come from England to Holland and were now ready to move on again.

"We do not go in search of riches," they declared, "but to start a colony where we can worship God as we think right."

The day came for the strong and brave Pilgrims to sail from Holland to the New World. Their loved ones and neighbors came down to the ship "Speedwell" to bid them good-bye. Many of them could not keep back the tears, for they knew that they would never see again those who were leaving. The minister knelt down and asked God to keep all of them safe until they should meet again. The brave soldier Captain Miles Standish went on board, too. He was going to train the men to be soldiers in the New World and help protect them from any enemies they might find in their new home.

First the ship sailed to England, where they met another ship, the "Mayflower." Then the two ships, the "Speedwell" and the "Mayflower," set sail together. But the "Speedwell" began to leak. It had to be taken back to England to be repaired. Again they started off—and again they had trouble with the "Speedwell." This time

Those Who Dared

the men declared the ship was unfit for the long trip to the New World.

"Let us go on the 'Mayflower' with our friends," begged the Pilgrims on the leaking ship. Many of them were taken on board the "Mayflower," until at last the captain said, "There is room for no more. The decks are too crowded. The cabins are packed. It will not be safe for another to come." When he counted them, he found he had one hundred and two on board. Of this number there were twenty-one women and twenty-eight children.

On The Ocean

The voyage across the ocean was not the trip of pleasure it is today. It took the Pilgrims more than two months to make the crossing, which is now made in less than a week.

Sometimes the tiny "Mayflower" tossed and rolled like a log upon the waters.

The story is told that when the ship was pitching at its worst a passenger, John Howland, came on deck and fell into the ocean. One of the ropes on deck had also been tossed over by the rolling of the ship. John caught hold of the rope, but was dragged beneath the sea. It seemed that he would be drowned if he held on to the rope and lost if he let go. After a while someone saw him. The rope was pulled in and he was saved.

Think how the women and children suffered on this rough sea! Their sea-sickness was worse because they did not have fresh food as we have today on our ocean

CAPTAIN MILES STANDISH GOES ASHORE ON THE ROCKY COAST OF NEW ENGLAND TO FIND A GOOD PLACE FOR THE MAYFLOWER PILGRIMS TO SETTLE

liners. They did not have comfortable rooms. Probably the only fire on board the ship was one for cooking, built on a flat hearth on the deck.

The weary Pilgrims welcomed the sight of land. They recognized Cape Cod from the map which Captain John Smith had made of New England. When they came into a good harbor, "they fell upon their knees" there on the "Mayflower" and gave thanks to God for their safe voyage. This was in November, 1620, but they did not leave the "Mayflower" for several weeks.

Those Who Dared
PLYMOUTH, THE NEW HOME

"It is not safe for your wives and children to go ashore," Captain Miles Standish advised the men. "Come, let us go first and see what kind of land this is."

More than one party was sent out before they found a place suited for a settlement. At last, one of the parties returned and the men said, "We have found a place for a fort and a town. There is a good harbor. Around this is cleared land, and the drinking water is good."

A few days later, the Mayflower came to a landing place which they named Plymouth, for the port in faraway England from which they had sailed. Other settlers went ashore. They too liked the site. From a high hill they could see all the country around. They thought it would be a safe place to settle.

Today one may stand on this hill, look below at Plymouth Rock, and see how wisely the Pilgrims chose their new home.

THE INDIANS

Unlike the colonists in Jamestown, the Pilgrims were not disturbed by the Indians during that first winter.

To protect themselves from the savages, if any should come, the new settlers formed a guard of soldiers. It was the duty of these men to keep their guns clean and ready for use at a moment's notice. Miles Standish was their captain.

To make their homes safer, they mounted, on high places, the five cannons they had brought from England.

SAMOSET, A FRIENDLY INDIAN, COMES TO VISIT THE PILGRIMS

SAMOSET AND SQUANTO, FRIENDS OF THE PILGRIMS

One day in the spring, the Pilgrims heard the cry, "Welcome!" There, ready to enter their town hall, stood an Indian whose name they found to be Samoset. He had learned some English from fishermen who had come to this coast. He was quite willing to talk as fast as he could find words.

He said he lived a day's journey from them by sea and five days by land.

He told the whites that a plague or great sickness had killed or driven away the Indians from that section.

After their visitor had spent the day, the Pilgrims wished he would leave, but he was not in a hurry. That

WHEN THE PILGRIMS WENT TO CHURCH, THEY TRUSTED GOD AND KEPT THEIR POWDER DRY

The Pilgrims

night he slept in a house, which they guarded carefully. The next morning when he left the settlers gave him presents.

A few days later Samoset returned with four other Indians. One of these, Squanto, proved to be a great friend to the whites. He lived with them and taught them to raise corn as the Indians did.

Samoset brought news that Massasoit, ruler of the near-by Indians, was coming on a visit to the settlers.

THE COMING OF THE INDIAN CHIEF

Soon the chief, Massasoit, with about sixty warriors, appeared. The Indians stopped on a hill near the settlement. Neither the English nor the Indians could decide which would trust the other. This was a very serious time. The Pilgrims did not want to make any mistake. Upon this visit might depend the friendship of their neighbors.

After a time the Pilgrims sent to Massasoit two knives and a chain with a jewel in it. With the gift went the message that the white men wished to be friends and trade with the Indians. Squanto did the talking because he understood and spoke English very well.

Massasoit decided to come nearer. With about twenty unarmed men, he came forward and was met by Captain Miles Standish with some of his men. They led their royal guest to an unfinished cabin spread with rugs. Here he was received by John Carver, the Pilgrim governor.

After the greetings were over, there was friendly

ON THE FIRST THANKSGIVING DAY, IN 1621, MANY FRIENDLY INDIANS WERE GUESTS OF THE PILGRIMS AND BROUGHT DEER AND WILD TURKEYS TO THE FEAST

talk. Then a treaty between the Indians and Pilgrims was signed. This said they would live in friendship and help each other in case of war with unfriendly people.

The First Thanksgiving

The Indians kept their treaty, and when fall came, the natives and the new settlers had their Thanksgiving dinner together.

The Indians brought five deer, which they gave to Miles Standish and the new governor, William Bradford. Governor Carver had died during the summer.

The Pilgrims

The women of Plymouth cooked the dinner in big fire-places over red-hot coals. Kettles and pots hung from a bar across the chimney. Other kettles and pans with long legs were set on the coals of fire.

The meat was hung by a chain so that it could be turned while it roasted near a hot blaze.

If the day was warm enough, the dinner for so many people was probably served out of doors on long tables, around which the guests sat on benches without backs. How different this was from a Thanksgiving scene of today!

CHAPTER VI

NEW YORK: HENRY HUDSON SAILS FROM THE WEEPERS' TOWER OF AMSTERDAM

Long ago before steamships were used, life at sea was one of great peril. But the seamen of Holland were among the bravest and boldest, ready to go out into unknown waters, unafraid of the terrors of the deep.

In those days of great danger, women and children knew the sorrows of the sea. Many husbands and fathers left home never to return. At the wharf in Amsterdam, one of the big cities of Holland, is a tower called the Weepers' Tower, because there, in the olden days, women and children said good-bye with tears to men going away to sea.

About two years after the settlers came to Jamestown, Henry Hudson sailed from the Weepers' Tower in Amsterdam. With him was his young son, John Hudson, and a crew of hearty sailors. They sailed on the "Half-Moon"—a ship as bold as was the red, red lion with golden mane which guarded the bow, a ship as bright as the gay flag of orange, white, and blue, which fluttered in the breeze. A striking ship it was, with its high points at the front and rear giving the vessel the shape of a half-moon. A bright sight it made with its many flags streaming as it sailed out of the harbor of Amsterdam.

New York: Henry Hudson

Henry Hudson was an Englishman, but a company of Dutch merchants hired him to find a shorter northern way to China. This was why Henry Hudson with his young son sailed northward from the Weepers' Tower that day in 1609. In those times merchants, traders, and seamen often sent or took their young sons off on the ships to learn their business or trade.

In the north Henry Hudson and his men met stubborn ice, through which they could not pass. Hudson did not want to go back to Holland and disappoint the Dutch East India Company. He had heard from his friend, Captain John Smith, of a strait, a narrow passage of water, in the New World, which the Captain thought might be a shorter way to China. Hudson talked this over with his crew. Then he turned the "Half-Moon" westward towards America.

Here they neared several points of land before they came into a lovely harbor, later known as New York Bay.

The ship anchored. Indians came aboard. They looked at the cannon. They were filled with awe and wonder at this strange ship of the white men. Perhaps this was the reason Henry Hudson was quite willing to have the Indians visit the "Half-Moon." He wanted them to fear the whites.

But the savages soon lost their awe and fear. The next day when Hudson sent men out to explore the waters around them, one of their number was killed by the Indians.

HENRY HUDSON, IN HIS SEARCH FOR A "NORTHWEST PASSAGE" TO CHINA SAILS THE "HALF-MOON" UP THE RIVER THAT NOW BEARS HIS NAME

After this the explorers watched the savages more closely.

During the lovely September days Henry Hudson sailed on up the "River of Steep Hills" which now bears his name. Near the present city of West Point he found the Indians very kind and friendly. Fur trading was carried on between the natives and the Dutch.

Henry Hudson went on shore with an old chief and visited him in his round house built of bark. Both sat on mats and ate out of red wooden bowls. The chief invited Hudson to spend the night. When he hesitated, the Indians broke their arrows and threw them into the fire to show they would do him no harm.

Henry Hudson sailed up the river to a place not far from the present city of Albany. Still he had not found

New York: Henry Hudson

waters which would take him to the Pacific. How disappointed he was!

After four weeks in the New World, Hudson and his men sailed back home. On the way, they came to England. There he was told he could not go back to Holland even to take his report to the Dutch East India Company. He had to stay and serve England. So he sent the "Half-Moon" on to Holland with his report. This pleased the Company, even though he had failed to find the shorter northern passage.

The Dutch East India Company were good traders. They were glad to know where they could find rich furs. These would bring them in gold as did the spices and silks of the far East. They decided to send trading vessels to the New World and there build up a fur trade with the Indians.

Hudson's Men Turn Against Him

England was proud of Henry Hudson. Now he was placed in command of an English ship. This was called the "Discovery," for Hudson still had faith that he would discover the northern route to China.

With high hopes, Hudson set sail once more. Again, he took his young son, John, with him. This time he decided to sail around the northern shores of America, but troubles arose. His men were rough and would not obey orders. The "Discovery" ran into great blocks of ice in unknown waters. This he thought must surely be the Pacific Ocean. Still Henry Hudson went on and

HENRY HUDSON CAST ADRIFT IN COLD NORTHERN WATERS

on, dodging the ice until he himself knew he had made another mistake.

Then his men were angry. Even the officers refused to obey him. He put others in charge whom he thought he could trust, only to find that all the men were now dissatisfied. Winter was coming. Food was getting scarce. The ice closed in on them. They could not hope to move for months.

Henry Hudson was greatly troubled. He felt for the safety of his men and his own son, so far from home and food. The men were brave. They ate what they could get. They broke the ice and fished. They were glad to see the first signs of spring. But it was June before the "Discovery" could turn around and set sail again.

Hudson wished to go on with his voyage. But the sailors had stood all they could. They rose against him.

64

New York: Henry Hudson

They bound their commander. He was taken from his ship and placed in a small boat. His son, John, and some sick sailors were lowered into the boat with him. But Hudson had at least one loyal friend. A carpenter on the ship would not leave his captain. With a gun, some powder, an iron pot, and a little meal, he joined Henry Hudson in the tiny boat. Then the "Discovery" sailed away to England, leaving Henry Hudson, his son, and the sick sailors there among the broken ice of the bay.

No one knows the rest of the story. But Henry Hudson will never be forgotten, for Hudson Bay and Hudson River bear his name.

Dutch Trading Posts and Early Settlers

In less than a year after the "Half-Moon" returned to Holland, Dutch traders were making their way across the ocean to the Hudson River. Fur trade with the Indians grew rapidly. The savages were eager to sell not only furs but even their land for beads, knives, and other trinkets.

Trading posts had to be built. One was located near the present city of Albany. Another was built near the mouth of the Hudson River. This they called New Amsterdam, after the Amsterdam they knew so well in Holland. You see the early settlers loved their mother country and they wanted to make their new home like the one they had known in the old world.

The trading post at New Amsterdam soon grew to be quite a little town. Long low houses were built with the

THE DUTCH BURGHERS OF NEW AMSTERDAM WOULD SIT IN PERFECT SILENCE, PUFFING THEIR PIPES, WITH HALF-SHUT EYES, AND "THINKING OF NOTHING FOR HOURS TOGETHER"

roofs made of bark and grass. There was a tall flag-pole, upon which floated the gay Dutch flag. Near by was the stone fort built to protect the Dutch from the Indians.

As time passed, the homes of the settlers looked more and more like the homes in Holland. The Dutch loved color; so there were gay flower-beds of red tulips and other bright flowers.

In time they had Dutch wind-mills, with their great arms covered with white cloth, just as the people had back home. There were street-lamps hung on a pole at night from every seventh house. There was a night watchman, too. He carried a lamp as he walked up and

New York: Henry Hudson

down and through the town from dark to dawn, as he called out the hour, "Nine o'clock and all is well," or "Midnight and all is quiet," "Five o'clock, a fog and cloudy morning."

The Dutch were a happy people. They were thrifty and worked hard; yet they were gay. In the summer they sat around the doorstep and talked with their neighbors. In the winter they gathered around the large open fire in their homes and talked and told stories. What lovely stories they could tell to children! The boys and girls had a much happier time than did the Pilgrim children. There were many feasts and holidays. The women were good cooks and gave dinners and parties in their homes. The men liked to sit and smoke after their meals. They did not talk as much as the women, but they played games and rolled nine-pins on the greens.

But happy as the Dutch were in their homes and with their neighbors, they had their troubles. They quarreled with their governors. We are told that one minister became so angry with the governor that when he preached he abused the governor from the pulpit. When the governor heard what the minister said, he ordered his soldiers to line up beneath the windows of the church on the next preaching day. When the people came to church they were surprised to see the armed soldiers guarding each window.

The minister knew that his people liked him better than they did the governor. He was not afraid of the soldiers; so he began to abuse the governor worse than ever.

Those Who Dared

"Bum! bum! bum!" beat the soldier drummers on their drums.

"Bang! bang!! bang!!!" went the soldiers' guns. Still the minister said hard things about the governor.

OLD SILVER NAILS

One of the strangest and sternest of the Dutch governors was old Peter Stuyvesant called "Old Silver Peg-Leg" or "Old Silver Nails."

"I shall be like a father over his children," promised Peter Stuyvesant when he came to New Amsterdam as governor.

But the settlers soon found that their governor was acting like a very stern father. He ruled everyone, even the oldest, as he stumped about the town.

He had been a soldier, and while fighting he had lost a leg. In its place, he wore a wooden peg-leg. He often said he was prouder of his wooden leg than he was of all his other limbs put together. And no one doubted him, for around his peg-leg there were silver bands, put on with silver nails, which glistened as he walked.

The Dutch boys and girls looked at their governor in awe. They, like their fathers and mothers, feared the stern old soldier who called meetings to order by thumping on the floor with his wooden leg.

The old governor found many troubles in the New World. His grown children objected to the stern rules. They wrote to their "High Mightinesses" who ruled back in the old country that they wished their governor's

New York: Henry Hudson

time of rule was over. Then, the trading posts were not managed to suit the strict governor, and he often had to visit them to see that his orders were carried out. There were Indian troubles, too.

One of the settlers, Van Dyck, had an orchard of ripe peaches. One day he found an old Indian squaw taking these peaches. He shot and killed the old woman.

Of course, this made the Indians furious. They vowed they would make the whites suffer for this, and they did. They attacked the whole Dutch settlement. The children fled in terror as they saw the Indians coming. There were sixty-four canoes, and each one was filled with warriors dressed and painted for the war-path. The alarm spread from home to home. The doors and windows were quickly shut and barred. This did not stop the Indians. They broke into the houses with terrible war-whoops. The screams of women and children were heard as they saw their own families killed. At each home the Indians stole whatever they wished and loaded it in their canoes.

Old Silver Nails was away at one of the forts when the attack was made. When he returned to the town, he was shocked and grieved at the sight. He was angry, too, not only with the Indians, but with the Dutchman, Van Dyck, who had caused all the trouble.

Now Old Silver Nails met the warriors and talked kindly to them. Later on he got them to make a treaty of peace, but this did not last.

The settlers repaired their homes after this Indian at-

Those Who Dared

tack. The town began to grow. Streets were laid out and named. Ships came into the harbor each year from the mother country and carried back thousands of dollars worth of furs to New Amsterdam. The settlers bought better furniture, china, and other goods. The homes were built larger and there were more of them. Old Silver Nails was proud of his town, but he was not proud of the small stone fort with its three small cannons.

"The fort is too small," he declared as he stumped around it. Then he wrote to their "High Mightinesses" to send more money to enlarge the fort.

But the men in the old country did not agree with Old Silver Nails; neither did his people. So nothing was done.

Soon they found that their governor was wiser than they were. About this time, the English began to look with longing eyes at the wealth which the Dutch had gained from their fur trade with the Indians.

"You are on English territory," said the English to the Dutch. "This land is ours. Cabot discovered it." Cabot was an Italian, but he lived in England and worked for that country.

By this time, there were many English living in New Amsterdam. Old Silver Nails saw that the people were not satisfied and were becoming restless. This troubled him.

Again came the cry, "Indians! Indians! They have gone on the war-path. Flee, flee for your lives!"

Old Silver Nails hurried off to quiet the Indian chiefs. While he was away, a messenger came from New Am-

OLD SILVER-NAILS TEARS UP THE ENGLISH ORDER TO SURRENDER NEW AMSTERDAM

Those Who Dared

sterdam with more bad news. English war-ships were coming into the harbor at New Amsterdam.

Home hurried Old Silver Nails. The next morning after his return, ships flying the English flag entered the lower harbor.

Colonel Nicolls was in command of the fleet. He wrote an order to Governor Stuyvesant to surrender with all the forts and no one would be harmed.

Old Silver Nails wanted more time. He was a pitiful sight. There the old soldier stood in the fort, looking down upon his enemy. His silver peg-leg thumped as he marched back and forth ready to command his men to fire.

The people were frightened. One man spoke, "To fight is madness." But the governor in his rage tore up the English order to surrender.

Again someone called out, "The English say if we surrender, no one will be hurt."

The old governor saw that he was already whipped. He did not want men killed uselessly. "I would much rather be carried to my grave than to give up," groaned Old Silver Nails, as he consented to surrender.

Not one shot was fired. The Dutch turned over their rich lands to the English. New Amsterdam was given an English name. It was called New York in honor of the king's brother, the Duke of York.

CHAPTER VII

PENN'S WOODS

Did you ever play the game of Indian Chief? Once a boy lived near me who had an Indian suit. His coat was fringed in front and there was fringe around the bottom of it. He had a real head-dress, too, of red, blue, yellow, and purple feathers. And with it he wore real beaded moccasins just as the Indians wore long ago.

When the English came to America, though they were grown men, they had to play with the Indians in order to deal with them. You see, the Indian had a meaning for everything he saw, touched, or smelled. Every color had a meaning. For instance purple meant calm, peace, and contentment.

There were few Englishmen who could understand the ways of the Indians. They were not wise enough to know the simple child-like natives. They did not understand that they must know the Indian's language in order to win his friendship and help him. They must learn that his money was called wampum. They must learn which wampum, the purple or the white, was worth more than the other.

Wampum was made of strings of purple or white beads. Each bead was about a quarter of an inch long, and half as wide. The purple beads were made from the purple clam-shell. They were polished as smooth as glass and

Those Who Dared

strung together through a hole in the center. These strings of purple wampum were the Indian's gold. The white wampum was made from the white shells and this was the Indian's silver. The Indians often made belts of these beads, and their wealth was reckoned by the number of belts which they owned. Sometimes the belts were woven in patterns that had a special meaning and were sent as messages.

Though the Indians seemed like children to the Englishmen, they had honor, loyalty, and pride. There was one man who loved and understood them. His name was William Penn. His statue is standing today in the city of Philadelphia, which he founded long ago.

William Penn was born at Tower Hill, London. His father was then a captain, but later became an admiral in the King's Navy.

Penn always loved the quiet of the country, the songs of birds, and the gurgle of the tumbling streams. When a very little boy, he ran to tell his neighbors some happy news. "I am going to the country to live," he shouted. "We are all going to Essex to make our home."

When William was eleven years old, a strange thing happened to him. One day he was alone in his room. Suddenly, there shone around about him a strange light. He was not afraid, for at the same time a deep happiness filled his heart. He felt that God was there in the room with him, and that God had called him to lead a holy life.

We may think it was only a dream which William

Penn's Woods

Penn had, but it was so real to the boy that it influenced all the rest of his life.

When William Penn was older his father said, "Now you must go up to Oxford to college." You see, Admiral Penn wanted the best for his son. He wanted him to know the sons of the best people, too, for he wanted William to have a high position in society.

But William did not care for society. His friends at Oxford were not the boys who liked pleasure and dressed in fine clothes, but the serious boys like himself.

Then one day William Penn went to hear Thomas Loe preach. This man, who was then at Oxford, was called a Quaker. He taught that there was an Inner Light or the voice of God within everyone's heart. He taught that every man was worth the same in the sight of God. The Quakers dressed simply and refused to take their hats off to anybody—even to the King. William Penn became a Quaker.

He was sent from college because he would not go to the college church, in which he did not believe. His father was angry with his son when he was told of this.

"Now I shall send you to France," shouted Admiral Penn to William, "to learn to behave like a gentleman."

William studied and traveled abroad. He wore fine clothes and learned to speak French very well. His father was pleased with him when he returned home.

Then came a strange and terrible sickness in London. It was called the London Plague. Many people died. William Penn went to the country, and there he grew

Those Who Dared

serious again. He read his Bible and went often into the woods to pray.

His father could not bear to see William going back to his old ways of religion. He decided to send him again to Ireland to be with an old friend of his. Once more William was happy with his rich friends.

He went to stay on his father's estate in Ireland. And there in the beautiful country the old longing to help others came into his heart. He longed to help his Quaker friends, who were being cruelly treated.

Again he heard his old friend Thomas Loe preach. That night William Penn made up his mind for all time. He too would be a Quaker preacher. From that night, he would accept the joys and sorrows of his Quaker friends.

While William Penn was preaching, his friend George Fox was in America. When he returned to England he told Penn what a wonderful country there was in the New World. They both wished they could take all their Quaker brothers and sisters to that far-away land. There they could worship God without being persecuted. And so William Penn began to dream of a colony in the New World, a haven for all those who loved God, no matter what they believed.

The King owed William Penn money which belonged to his father. You see, Admiral Penn had died and his fortune was given to his son. William Penn now asked the King to give him land in the New World instead of the money which the King owed to his father, and the

Penn's Woods

King agreed. Land in the New World! William Penn was delighted. Now he could make his dreams come true. He could send his Quaker neighbors to his own colony in America.

The King also gave William Penn power to make the laws and to appoint men to help him rule the colony. Penn in turn was to give the King two skins of beavers and one-fifth of all the gold and silver found in the ground. Penn wished to name the home of his colony "Sylvania," which means "a land of trees," but the King named it "Pennsylvania," in memory of Penn's father.

William Penn started to Pennsylvania on his ship, the "Welcome," with one hundred of his Quaker neighbors. But smallpox broke out among his passengers and over one-third of them died at sea.

Soon after the colony landed, William Penn called the Indians together to make a treaty with them and to pay them for their lands.

The Treaty With the Indians At the Place of Kings

The Indians said an elm tree meant peace. The Indian kings used to meet under a great elm near where the city of Philadelphia stands today. There under the elm they met in silence while they smoked their long peace-pipes. There they held great feasts after the warriors had won their games and races. They called this meeting place "Shack-a-maxon!—The Place of Kings."

One day more Indians than usual came to the Place

Those Who Dared

of Kings—for William Penn, the governor of Penn's Woods, was to meet them for the first time. But they did not call him Governor Penn. They called him "Onas," the Indian word for pen.

Famous pictures have been painted of Penn's meeting with the Indians, but we have to imagine what really happened there. The Indians had been coming since the rising of the sun. They sat in the shade of the great elm, the hickory, the walnut, and the cedar trees.

The chiefs seated themselves around the elm in a half-circle, like the new moon. Taminent, their great chief, sat in the middle. Around him sat his oldest warriors, in a circle too. The young braves sat behind the older ones and behind them sat the squaws and the little children—all keeping the half-circle like a new moon.

The birds, we are told, were singing a sweet welcome too. The red rays of the sun made the paint on the faces of the warriors shine and glisten. The soft breeze made their gay plumes and feathers dance upon their head-dresses. It was a colorful crowd which William Penn and his friends found there in the early morning.

When Onas (William Penn) came, the Indians arose. The spark was put under the council fires. That was a signal for the chiefs to go apart to prepare themselves for the real ceremony—that of a treaty of peace between themselves and the Quakers.

The Quakers gathered together on one side of the great council fire. Then the Indians formed on the other, still keeping the half-moon curve.

Penn's Woods

Then Taminent, the great chief, came forward. He held in his hands a crown made of oak leaves. He took a great thorn and held it as if it were a precious jewel. Indeed to the Indians it meant more than a jewel—for the thorn meant power. Taminent stuck the thorn into the crown of leaves. He lifted the crown high into the air for a moment before he placed it upon his own head. This crown was sacred to them. When the chief wore it no person could be harmed. All must be at peace.

The silence deepened. Only the singing of the birds broke the stillness. The warriors came before their chief and then carried bows and arrows and hid them.

Taminent stood still, self-crowned lord of the Indians, of the hills, of the caves, of the distant mountains, and of the near-by sea. He spoke, saying, "My White Brother, the hour is come. We have gathered at your call. Speak, we are ready to hear."

Then William Penn, the kindly Quaker went forward, holding a white paper in his hand. He said words like these:

"Brothers, there lives within us that Great Spirit God. The sun shines above us, and the stars of night march in their courses. I will not call you my children or my brothers, because parents punish their children and brothers disagree. We are a body, one body of the same flesh and blood and heart. The body cannot be divided. We are one body—a body in two parts, but the same body."

The treaty declared that from that day, the Turkeys,

WILLIAM PENN'S TREATY WITH THE INDIANS AT SHACK-A-MAXON

the Turtles, and the Wolves (names which the Indian tribes called themselves), should be friends forever with the white children of Onas, that all roads should be free and open to each other, that the doors of the white men should be open to the red men, and doors of the red men always open to the white men, that they should not speak evil of each other, and they should both correct any evil reports of the other, that should any white man wrong a red man, or a red man wrong a white, the case should be tried by twelve men—six from the white men and six from the Indian tribes. William Penn told the Indians that this treaty should be read by them as they sat around their council fires and handed down to their children's children.

Penn's Woods

"Brothers," said a Quaker when William Penn had finished reading the treaty, "you have heard. Will you keep this treaty with us?" The Indians answered, "As long as the streams shall flow and the sun and the moon endure."

"You will be always friendly?" asked the Quaker.

"As long as the streams shall flow and the sun and the moon endure," chanted the Indians.

"All your roads shall be open to the white men?" asked the Quaker?

"As long as the streams shall flow and the sun and the moon endure."

"And all doors shall be kept open to each other?" asked the Quaker.

"As long as the streams shall flow and the sun and the moon endure."

And so we can picture the Indians chanting in promise to all parts of the treaty. Then the Indian Chief, Taminent, gave Onas a wampum belt—a beautiful one which had purple beads in it—the beads which meant peace. In the belt were woven two figures: one was an Indian; one was a white man. Their hands were clasped in friendship. This belt was carefully kept by William Penn, and we are told that when he went back to England he took it to the palace in London and showed it to the King and his court. It may now be seen in Philadelphia.

The Indians gave Penn corn and other tokens of their friendship.

Then William Penn gave presents to the Indians, too.

Those Who Dared

There was no oath to this treaty. It was the only one "never sworn to and never broken by either." The seal to the treaty was in their hearts.

After the treaty there were all kinds of games played by the Indians. William Penn joined in them. He was as nimble and quick as the Indian braves.

Soon the squaws called both the Indians and the Quakers to eat the great feast which they had prepared. There were roast turkeys, venison, fish, corn, and fruits.

William Penn laid out his city near this Place of Kings under the great elm. He called it Philadelphia, which means "Brotherly Love." William Penn and his neighbors were friends of the Indians. The English owned the land, as a gift from the King of England, but they always paid the Indians for the land on which they planted and built. They knew that the lands had belonged to the Indians first.

William Penn wanted men and women to come and live in his colony, and he let them worship God as they pleased. Many Germans came to live there, and many Dutch and Swedish people from the colonies to the north. The Quakers soon mixed English words with the German as they tried to talk to their German neighbors. The Germans did the same. They spoke neither English nor German. Yet they could understand each other. They called this speech "Pennsylvania Dutch."

William Penn lived a life of service for others. Penn's Woods, or Pennsylvania, is now one of the greatest and richest states in our Union.

CHAPTER VIII

A FRIEND TO THE FRIENDLESS

James Oglethorpe was shocked. His friend, Robert Castell, was in Fleet Prison, a debtors' prison in London. As soon as he could, James Oglethorpe hurried off to the prison to see if he could help his friend.

He had never thought very much about prisons. He had been used to a comfortable home as a boy. His father had been a major general in the English army and his mother was called "Lady Oglethorpe."

James went to school at Oxford, but he soon left there and joined the army of Prince Eugene, who was fighting the Turks in Europe. In this war he was a brave soldier. At the time of our story, he was very active in the public life of his country.

James Oglethorpe arrived at the prison. He asked to see his friend. "How glad I am to see you, James!" said Robert. "But I am sorry for you to see me in this foul place."

"Tell me what has brought you here, Robert?" asked James. "Perhaps, I can find a way to get you out."

"Alas! Alas!" replied Robert bitterly. "I made some debts which I could not pay on time."

Do you mean to tell me that you are kept in this dirty prison because you have not money to pay at once an honest debt?" inquired James Oglethorpe.

OGLETHORPE'S FRIEND, IN PRISON FOR DEBT, BEGS THE JAILOR NOT TO MOVE HIM TO THE "COMMON SIDE," WHERE PRISONERS HAVE TO SLEEP ON THE FLOOR

"Aye," Robert replied, "and if I did not have a few coins to give as presents to the warden, I should be thrown into the Common Side, which is far worse than this."

"And pray what is the Common Side? How could it be worse than this, Robert? The very air here is sickening!"

"The Common Side is the place where men are put who cannot pay for beds," Robert explained. The poor fellows sleep upon the floor, with many prisoners who are ill and dying."

Friend to the Friendless

After James Oglethorpe left, the warden paid a visit to Robert Castell. But Robert did not have any money to give the warden on this visit, and the warden was very angry.

"You shall be turned over to Corbett," ordered the warden. "He has charge of the other part of the prison."

"Surely you would not send me there, where smallpox is raging!" pleaded Robert. "I have never had the disease and would surely die."

"If there is no money to keep you here, you will be sent there," replied the warden.

And in spite of his pleas and those of others, Robert was thrown into the prison filled with smallpox.

The unhappy man was already ill. He caught smallpox and died in a few days. With his last breath, he called the warden his murderer.

James Oglethorpe was sad indeed. He determined to help other men who were unjustly imprisoned, as Robert Castell had been. He was able, through his wealthy friends, to get a committee appointed to study the prisons. This committee found that good people, who were in debt through no fault of their own, shared the prison with those who had stolen or killed.

The committee then visited the warden and saw how cruel and unjust he had been. Although he was punished, the unhappy debtors were not freed.

James Oglethorpe could not forget the death of Robert Castell. He longed for a place where men who were honest could work and pay off their debts.

Those Who Dared

He began to talk to other friends. He told them about a prison where 657 men were crowded into a space not large enough for half that number. He told them the sad story of Robert Castell.

Then James Oglethorpe thought of a plan. He talked to wealthy men and got them interested. They asked King George to let them settle a colony in the New World. Twenty-one men agreed to be the trustees for the new colony. James Oglethorpe was to be their governor without any pay. They called the colony Georgia in honor of their king.

James Oglethorpe and the trustees raised the money to pay for the boat, the crew, and the debtors' passage on the ship to America.

Each debtor was to be given fifty acres of land in the new colony. He did not have to buy it or pay rent. There he could raise crops and pay off his debts.

Then came the time to choose the debtors who were to go. How hard it was to refuse the pleas of those poor men who wished to be taken to America! At last thirty-five men were told that they could take their families to Georgia.

Among these men were carpenters, bricklayers, farmers, and laborers.

James Oglethorpe and the trustees bought tools and supplies to be used in the new colony.

On November 6, 1732, the debtors and their families were happy to board the good ship "Anne" and sail for their new home.

Friend to the Friendless
A Home for Debtors

The "Anne" arrived in the harbor at Charleston, South Carolina, after two months at sea. James Oglethorpe called his people together and they gave thanks to God for their safe voyage.

Their landing was very different from that of the colonists at Jamestown and Plymouth, more than a hundred years before. Then there were no friendly settlers to welcome the newcomers or to advise them in their strange new homes. Now, Oglethorpe went ashore and was received by the Governor of South Carolina and his council. They were delighted to know that another English colony was to be their neighbor. The new colony would help to protect them from the Spaniards in Florida.

The Governor of South Carolina ordered the King's pilot to guide the "Anne" along the sea-coast to the Savannah River. This river was the boundary line between South Carolina and Georgia. Oglethorpe and his colonists sailed up the river about twenty miles. There they found a suitable spot for a town.

The men went to work at once and cut from the trees branches with which they made tree-tents to be used as homes for their families until better houses could be built. Governor Oglethorpe called the place Savannah.

Oglethorpe had many plans for the new colony. He wanted them to live in peace with the Indians. He did not want whiskey or rum in the colony. He reminded the settlers how other colonies had unwisely given to

OGLETHORPE'S COLONISTS BUILDING THE TOWN OF SAVANNAH

the Indians rum, or "fire water," as the natives called it. Neither did Oglethorpe wish to have slaves among his people. Yet he wanted all to be busy. He planned to raise silkworms on the mulberry trees which grew in this climate. He thought that this would give work to the women, children, and old people. Workers were brought from Italy to show how the worms should be fed and how the silk should be wound from the cocoons. Oglethorpe and the trustees believed that the raising of raw silk would help the colonists to prosper.

Governor Oglethorpe planned for beauty as well as the comfort of his people. Public gardens were laid out

The First Settlers

in the center of the town. Shade trees, fruit trees, vines, shrubs, and even cotton plants and coffee bushes had a place on these grounds. The walks were bordered by orange trees, and in the squares were large numbers of mulberry trees.

Oglethorpe planned his colony not only for unfortunate debtors, but also for more fortunate people who wished to start homes in the New World. Many came there, too, who wished to be allowed to worship God in their own way.

Many of Oglethorpe's plans did not succeed, but his settlement, Savannah, was the beginning of Georgia, a home for debtors and for many other people. Georgia was the last of the thirteen English colonies which the early settlers planted on the Atlantic coast from Florida to Maine.

THE LIBRARY

Stories in Other Books

"For England and the Queen," "What Sought They Thus Afar," in *These United States and How They Came to Be*, by Gertrude Hartman.

"Jamestown the Cradle of America," "An Indian King and a Princess," in *The Story of Virginia*, by Carrie Hunter Willis and Lucy S. Saunders.

"John Smith the Founder of Virginia," in *Founders of Our Country*, by Fanny E. Coe.

"Captain John Smith," in *Ten Great Adventurers*, by Kate Dickinson Sweetser.

"Pocahontas, the Little Indian Princess," "The First Thanksgiving Day in New England," "How Pilgrim Chil-

Those Who Dared

dren Went to Meeting in Winter," *American History Stories for Very Young Readers*, by Eva March Tappan.

"A Visit to a Tobacco Plantation," "On the Way to Lynnhaven Bay and the Oyster Beds," in *Then and Now in Dixie*, by Rose Mortimer Ellzey MacDonald.

"The First Governor of Boston," "William Penn and the Indians," in *Stories of Great Americans for Little Americans*, by Edward Eggleston.

"After the Storm," "Wash Day," "Finding the Corn," "Attacked by the Savages," "Miles Standish," in *Mary of Plymouth*, by James Otis [Kaler].

"Squanto, the Corn Planter," "At The First Thanksgiving," in *History Stories For Primary Grades*, by John Walter Wayland.

"Henry Hudson and the Half-Moon," in *Great Moments in Exploration*, by Marion Florence Lansing.

"The Founder of Virginia," "Miles Standish, Captain of Plymouth," "New Netherlands, Old New York," "A Quaker in the New World," "The Father of Georgia," in *Founders of Our Country*, by Fanny E. Coe.

"Captain John Smith Saves Jamestown," "The Beginning of New England," "The Beginning of New York," "William Penn's Colony of Pennsylvania," in *Our Nation Begins*, by Eugene C. Barker, William E. Dodd, and Walter P. Webb.

Self-Testing Games

Write in a column the numbers 1 to 10. After each number place the word or words that make true the sentence having the same number. Each correct sentence counts 2.

1. English merchants formed two companies called the ―― Company and the ―― Company.
2. The first colony which was sent out by the Company had their written orders in a ―― ――.
3. ―― ―― commanded the flag-ship.
4. The voyage was a ―――― one.

The First Settlers

5. Men looked to —— —— for advice.
6. At last Smith was put —— ——.
7. The ships anchored at Cape Henry on —— ——.
8. After a short time they sailed up the James River and settled at ——.
9. Captain Smith was tried and allowed to take his place in the ——.
10. ——, a little Indian Princess, became a good friend of the white settlers.

The highest possible score is 20. Count your score.

Game II

This is the game of Who. Write the numbers 1 to 10. After each number write the answer to the question having the same number. Each correct answer counts 2.

WHO

1. Went to Holland to worship as they believed they should?
2. Was a well-known English soldier who came with the Pilgrims to the New World?
3. Made a map of the New England coast?
4. Among the Indians was a great friend to the Pilgrims?
5. Made a treaty with the Indians that was never broken?
6. Sailed from the Weepers' Tower of Amsterdam to the present state of New York?
7. Would not leave his captain, Henry Hudson?
8. Was called "Old Silver Nails"?
9. Changed the name of New Amsterdam to New York?
10. Was known as "A Friend to the Friendless"?

What is your score? The highest possible score is 20.

Choose Something to Do

1. Divide your class into four groups. Let each group select and dramatize a scene; one from the story of the settlers at Jamestown; one from the story of the Pilgrims; one from the stories of Henry Hudson and New York; one from

Those Who Dared

the stories of Penn's Wood; and one from the stories about Georgia.

2. Make riddles about the following people: Captain John Smith, Pocahontas, Powhatan, Captain Newport, Miles Standish, Squanto, Henry Hudson, Admiral Penn, William Penn, Robert Castell, and James Oglethorpe. Let your class-mates guess the answer to your riddles.

3. Draw two pictures, one showing Jamestown, the other Plymouth. What differences do your pictures show in the beginning of the two settlements?

4. Perhaps you can get some silkworms for your schoolroom. You can care for the worms and see the cocoons of silk, as the people of Georgia did long ago.

PART III
CHILDREN OF LONG AGO.

CHAPTER IX

A LITTLE GIRL OF LONG AGO

1710

Little Catalina Schuyler was seven years old when she was left an orphan. Colonel Peter Schuyler carried her to his home which was named The Flats, near Albany. There Catalina found a warm welcome. Her aunt and cousins did all they could to make the little girl happy.

Catalina loved her uncle. Colonel Schuyler was very brave. He was kind to the Indians with whom he traded. They said he was always fair and never took more beaver or mink-skins than was fair. They called him "Brother Peter." They said, "Brother Peter never speaks without thinking."

Colonel Schuyler had just returned from England when Catalina went to live in The Flats. She liked to hear him tell about taking four Indian chiefs with him to England. He said they had been like children. They were pleased with everything—their trip on the "floating palace," as the ship was called; their visit to the Queen, the presents they received, and the attention that was paid to them.

The Queen received Colonel Schuyler, too, with favor. She gave him presents and offered to make him a knight.

"And are you a knight, Uncle Schuyler?" asked Catalina eagerly.

Those Who Dared

"No, no little Catalina," replied her uncle as he shook his head and laughed. "I told Her Majesty, Queen Anne, it might cause unkind feelings and vain thoughts in the family. I am no better than my brothers."

Catalina was sorry he had refused the knighthood. She felt he deserved to be more than a knight.

"Now, it is time for your lessons," said Colonel Schuyler.

Catalina soon learned to read. She wanted to please her Uncle and Aunt Schuyler. She was determined to learn the long hard words in the big Dutch Bible so that she could surprise her uncle. After her lessons Catalina sewed or knitted stockings. Her aunt also taught the little girl to embroider and cross-stitch a sampler. She learned to polish the glass and pewter too, for all little girls had to know how to be good housekeepers.

Catalina liked the outdoor life at her uncle's home. In the spring the men dug and spaded the big garden. Then it was turned over to the women. Beans, celery, carrots, beets, and potatoes were planted.

There was a large flower garden too at The Flats, like those in Europe.

Harvest time was happy for the early settlers. The Schuyler master, mistress, servants, and children went down, like their neighbors, to see the grain harvested.

The Schuyler barn was the biggest in all that part of New York. Catalina watched the driver guide the team and wagon up the sloping platform, through the two huge doors, and into the middle of the barn. The men from

A Little Girl of Long Ago

the top of the loaded wagon forked the hay above into the dark loft.

It was fun for the children to catch the grasshoppers jumping on the mounds of fresh hay, to watch the butterflies fluttering about, or to listen to the chirp of the crickets.

In the lower part of the barn were stalls for the cows and horses. On one side there were huge box-like chests, which held the corn, wheat, barley, and oats. Catalina and the children dipped their hands into the grain as their elders did, and threw it to the waiting chickens, ducks, and turkeys. Birds, too, darted down and ate their part.

The grain was threshed in this big barn and then was stored away for winter use.

On New Year's Eve, Catalina saw a strange custom. A little three-year-old son of a slave was brought into the Great House of her Schuyler cousins. This little slave was given to the Schuyler boy, who was about the same age. The little white boy gave a pair of shoes and a piece of money to the little Negro boy. From that day, the little Negro was the slave of his little white master.

Sometimes the same ceremony was repeated, only it would be a little Negro girl who was given to a little white girl.

The little slaves then spent most of their time in the Great House. They were good playmates and friends as well as servants.

The parents of these Negro children were slaves whom

CATALINA'S UNCLE, PETER SCHUYLER, TRADING WITH THE INDIANS FOR FURS. THE SKINS, CAREFULLY FOLDED, MAY BE SEEN TIED IN A NEAT BUNDLE BESIDE THE BOX

the Dutch ships had brought from Africa and sold to Catalina's uncle and his neighbors. These Negro men and women were taken into the homes of the more wealthy settlers. There they were to cook, clean, and later to spin and sew. They were told about God and many of them became Christians.

Colonel Schuyler made quite a pet of Catalina. He often took her to the Indian village near The Flats. She learned to speak the Indians' language as they brought their beaver, and mink, and other skins to show. While

A Little Girl of Long Ago

her uncle traded with the Indian men, Catalina talked to the squaws and children. She watched the brown, nimble fingers of the Indian maids as they embroidered the soft deer-skin with wampum beads. They made belts and baskets too. Catalina loved the gay colors of the baskets. The Indians were the only ones who knew how to make these colors from the bark of trees or from vegetables and weeds which grew everywhere.

On Catalina's visits to the Indian village, there were many other things to see. There were queer strong switch brooms made by tying birch switches together. There were wooden dishes and bowls carved from soft wood and painted in gay colors.

When Catalina grew older she taught the Indians, and they were devoted to her, as they were to her uncle.

CHAPTER X

JACK AND PATSY CUSTIS AT MOUNT VERNON

Jack Custis was a very proud little boy. He was going to ride his horse without anyone to hold his bridle. Colonel Washington, his stepfather, had taught him to "sit his horse like a gentleman" and had given him permission to ride without a groom. Colonel Washington felt the saddle straps to see that they were properly fastened. He watched Jack mount and then waved good-bye as the boy rode away.

Patsy, Jack's younger sister waved too. She was afraid the horse would throw her brother. Colonel Washington told her Jack was old enough now to ride alone. He could hold the reins and guide his horse as well as a man.

That made Patsy feel better. She knew her stepfather loved her brother "as his very own son." She followed Colonel Washington into the large stable. While he talked to the coachman, Patsy counted the horses in their stalls. There were four strong ones which pulled the great, heavy family coach in which the Colonel and Mrs. Washington, Jack, and herself rode to Pohick Church or to visit the Masons who lived at Gunston Hall, the next plantation. In one of the stalls a groom was currying Colonel Washington's favorite riding horse. When Patsy

GEORGE WASHINGTON, HIMSELF A FINE HORSEMAN, TAUGHT LITTLE JACK CUSTIS TO RIDE

saw the groom put a saddle on the horse, she knew that her stepfather was going to overtake Jack as he rode over the Mount Vernon plantation.

When Colonel Washington rode off, Patsy went into the garden where her mother was cutting flowers. Patsy loved the garden, with its odd-shaped beds, which were bordered with dwarf boxwood. Colonel and Mrs. Washington were constantly planting seeds and plants. The yellow jasmine was still blooming, and so was the scarlet honey-suckle, which was so sweet. Patsy could name many other flowers. There were mock orange, sour

Those Who Dared

orange, red spice berries, lavender, sweet william, and roses.

Patsy helped her mother carry the flowers. On their way to the house Mrs. Washington passed the "spinning house." She went in to see how the new wool was working up. Patsy went in too. She never was tired of watching the women spin the clean creamy wool into the heavy thread, or of listening to the whir of the spinning-wheels. Sometimes the colored women sang as they worked. Near by were the heavy wooden looms where the yarn thread was woven into thick cloth for winter clothes. Sometimes the wool was dyed before it was woven into cloth.

Mrs. Washington and Patsy next visited the large kitchen which was in the yard near the house. The cook showed them the bread and meats which the house-keeper had "measured out" for the day's meals. There were vegetables of all kinds ready to be cooked in the iron pots, in time for the two o'clock dinner.

Patsy helped her mother fill the vases with water. Then she had to study. Mrs. Lund Washington, the children's teacher, taught her to read and write. Her mother sat near and knitted. She herself taught her little daughter to sew, embroider, and to play on the spinet. After her lessons, Patsy sewed awhile.

A shadow fell across the door way. Patsy looked up to see Mammy standing in the door.

" 'Scuse me, Miss Martha," the elderly colored woman spoke to Mrs. Washington. "But Miss Patsy must be

Jack and Patsy Custis

tired of being still so long. Better let the child go outdoors with me and get some color in her cheeks."

"Yes, Mammy," agreed Mrs. Washington. "You may go now, Patsy. We will sew again tomorrow."

In every plantation home there was a mammy. She usually was a middle-aged or old Negro woman who had been reared in the mansion house. She nursed the children as babies, fed them, taught them to walk, sang them to sleep at night, dressed them and taught them "manners." No one held a higher place in the family than did "Mammy." She was loved by the father and mother as well as by the children themselves. Jack and Patsy loved their Mammy, who had lived with them during their father's life before they came to Mount Vernon.

Patsy and Mammy sat on the flag-stone porch at Mount Vernon. Patsy knew that the stones came from England when Colonel Washington made larger the old house which had come to him from his half-brother, Lawrence Washington. Patsy often counted the thirty-six heavy Windsor chairs which had been brought from England at the same time.

The Coming of the Packet Boat

"Look, Mammy," cried Patsy, "I see the packet boat! I do believe it is coming into the Mount Vernon landing."

"So it is, Miss Patsy," said Mammy as she shaded her eyes. "It is bringing Colonel's order, which should have been here three weeks ago!"

Those Who Dared

Patsy and Mammy walked down the long green sloping lawn to the wharf. The packet boat was making great waves in the Potomac River, which flows along the banks of the Mount Vernon plantation.

"And here comes the Colonel," said Mammy. "And there is Mr. Jack with him. He is a grown young man now—or so he thinks, riding a horse by himself."

Colonel Washington directed the unloading of many boxes. These were sent to the house before they were unpacked. Patsy and Jack could hardly wait for the men to open them.

The first large box held a spinet for Patsy. A smaller box was opened next. In it was a small well-made saddle of the finest leather for Master Jack. There were riding boots to match, a powder horn with silver trimmings, riding breeches, and a "laced-up" hat. There were books, toys, and tops, two dolls for Patsy, gloves, and several pairs of boots for both of them, handkerchiefs, coats, and dresses. There was a small Bible for each child, with their names printed in gold letters. Of course there were lovely dresses for Mrs. Washington, pins, lace collars, and other fine things which could not be bought in the colonies.

PLEASURES AT MOUNT VERNON

Life at Mount Vernon was full of pleasure as well as of work. Colonel Washington and his lovely wife were very hospitable. They enjoyed having their neighbors in for dinners, for dancing, and for tea. Mrs. Washington was pretty, graceful, and dignified, yet easy in her man-

Jack and Patsy Custis

ners with the younger people who often came to Mount Vernon. She served tea every afternoon whether there were guests or not, and Colonel Washington, riding from the fields, came in to have a cup of tea with her.

Colonel Washington had engaged Mr. Christian, the dancing master, to teach Jack and Patsy to dance. Sometimes the master spent the night with them when he came. Then a note was sent to invite the Masons to Mount Vernon for their dancing lesson. Colonel Washington often danced with the young people. He was fond of foxhunting and frequently took Jack with him. There were few dull days at Mount Vernon. Only one cloud hung over the home. Patsy, whom the servants called the "Little Dark Lady," was not strong.

JACK AND PATSY GROW OLDER

When Jack was fourteen, he was sent to Mr. Boucher, near Annapolis, Maryland, to be taught. Jack took with him his body servant who looked after his clothes and took care of his horse. Jack had made many friends, and when he went home for a vacation, he took Colonel Washington an invitation from one of his friends. It was from Jack's tutor, Mr. Boucher. He invited Colonel Washington, Mrs. Washington, Jack, and Patsy to visit him.

Colonel Washington, after talking it over with Mrs. Washington, decided to accept.

The horses and coach were sent across the river on a heavy flat-boat the night before and taken to Mr. Diggs's

WHEN THE WASHINGTON FAMILY TRAVELED, THEY WENT IN A "COACH AND FOUR"

stables which were on the Maryland shore of the Potomac River opposite Mount Vernon. Early the next morning, Colonel Washington and his family were taken across the river on a boat. They were met by Mr. Diggs, who "escorted" his friends to his comfortable home. There Mrs. Diggs was waiting to welcome them and give them a delicious hot Maryland breakfast.

After breakfast the friends talked for a while. Then Colonel Washington said they must be going if they were to reach Mr. Boucher's in time for dinner. The Washington coach was brought to the door, and after the Washingtons had promised to visit the Diggs family on the return journey, they said good-bye.

When the Washingtons arrived at Mr. Boucher's, they

Jack and Patsy Custis

found other guests awaiting them. Governor Eden of Maryland, with Colonel Calvert and his two lovely daughters, gave them a warm welcome.

What good times the young people had! Jack liked Eleanor Calvert better than any other girl he had ever met. She was fond of outdoor sports. There is a picture painted of her in a handsome riding habit and wearing a boy's hat which she wore when she went fox-hunting. Jack thought she was as beautiful in those clothes as she was when she wore the stylish silks and bonnets which came from London.

The Calverts had to go home before Sunday, but plans were made for visits and dinings at their home, Mount Airy, during the next week before the Washingtons returned to Mount Vernon.

Governor Eden asked Colonel Washington to drive with him to church in his phaëton. We are not told how the others went, but when there were services no one was excused from going to church unless one was sick.

The next spring the Calverts visited Mount Vernon. Jack could show the girls the fine horses. Perhaps they galloped over to Gunston Hall to see the Masons, or drove to Alexandria, or to Belvoir where the Fairfaxes lived. No doubt there were merry times at Mount Vernon with other guests who dropped in.

Last Days at Mount Vernon

The time came for Jack to go to college. He rode his horse, and his man-servant went along to look after

Those Who Dared

him. On his way, Jack stopped at Mount Airy to see Eleanor. Two days later Colonel Washington joined him and they rode to Philadelphia. Colonel Washington wanted Jack to see the largest city in the colonies. There they attended the theater and were invited to dinner with friends. From Philadelphia, they went to New York, where Jack entered King's College.

Jack was a fine young man, one of the finest in all Virginia. Though he had been brought up to have the best of everything, from gold buttons for his shirts and silver buckles for his shoes, to the finest riding horses, he was unspoiled. But Jack was not a student. He liked the out-of-doors; he liked riding to his hounds on a fox chase and the life of a plantation. He was homesick when he reached Philadelphia. He was more so when he arrived in New York. Yet he promised to stay. He wrote long letters to his mother and to Eleanor.

That summer Patsy was taken suddenly ill. She who had never been strong "entered into a more happy and peaceful place than she had ever known," wrote Colonel Washington to his friend.

The next winter Jack and Eleanor were married. Mrs. Washington did not feel she could go, but she urged Colonel Washington to go without her.

Though the groom was only nineteen and the bride just sixteen, the marriage was very happy, and years later their two children made Mount Vernon ring again with merriment.

CHAPTER XI

IN THE DAYS OF YOUNG JOHN QUINCY ADAMS AND ABBY ADAMS

One August morning there was great excitement at Braintree, the home of the Adams family near Boston. Mr. Adams was going on a long trip. He was going to Philadelphia, five hundred miles away.

"How long will it take papa to drive to Philadelphia?" John Quincy asked his mother, after Mr. Adams had gone to Boston to join the men who were going with him.

"It will take almost three weeks or a little less, John Quincy," replied Mrs. Adams. "That stage road is one of the best in the colonies."

"How did people know where to build the roads, mama?" asked John Quincy.

"Why, they followed the trails made by the Indians," Mrs. Adams told him.

"And where will papa eat and sleep?" Abby asked.

"Papa and the other men will stop at taverns along the way. They will have good food and sleep on feather beds like those we have at home. And now, Abby, it is time for you to help Patsie polish the pewter. And John, you must write your copy. Try to form your letters as your teacher does. Papa will expect you to write him a letter while he is in Philadelphia."

JOHN QUINCY ADAMS AND ABBY ADAMS WITH THEIR MOTHER AT THEIR HOME IN BRAINTREE, MASSACHUSETTS. JOHN QUINCY'S FATHER BECAME THE SECOND PRESIDENT OF THE UNITED STATES AND JOHN QUINCY HIMSELF THE SIXTH PRESIDENT

While the children were working at their tasks and baby Charles was asleep, Mrs. Adams got her yarn. Then she called her other maid to her.

"Susie," Mrs. Adams said, "we must get to the spinning today. There are blankets and all the heavy cloth to be woven before winter. You may use the best wool for the blankets. Are your big loom and wheel running smoothly?"

John Quincy and Abby Adams

"Yes, Mrs. Adams," replied Susie. "Will you weave the sheets today? The old ones will not stand much more washing."

"They are going fast," agreed Mrs. Adams. "Yes I will begin weaving sheets today and perhaps some towels and a table cloth."

When Abby had finished polishing the pewter and had dusted her mother's bedroom as usual, she wanted to play.

"No, you cannot go out yet, Abby," her mother told her. "You have not done a round on your knitting."

"Mama, I've dropped a stitch," Abby confessed. "I cannot get it back on the needle. Let me play until you are through weaving."

"No," replied her mother firmly but kindly. "One must work before one plays. Bring the knitting to me. I will show you how to pick up the stitches."

"Why Abby," Mrs. Adams said as she looked at the small stocking on which the little girl was knitting. "See, how ugly this top row looks beside the neat rows below. Pull out two rows. Then I will show you how to pick up the stitches again."

"You are doing very well for a little girl just beginning to knit," said Mrs. Adams. "When you have finished your stocking, I will give you wool to knit a pair of gloves for your papa."

"O, mama," cried Abby forgetting the dropped stitches, "I will take pains to do them neatly."

John Quincy studied with Mr. John Thaxter and

Those Who Dared

did real sums in arithmetic and read the history of the Old World. But Abby was taught by her mother. In those days, girls were not sent to school like boys. Girls were taught to read and write. They learned to sew, to embroider, to spin, and to weave. Abby learned all these things, and also how to cook, preserve fruit, and bake breads and pies like her mother.

Of all the things which her mother did Abby thought that soap-making was the most fun. She wondered how the soft pieces of meat and fat boiled with lye could get so hard and make lather. She liked to watch the maids as they stirred the great pots of boiling soap. Then it was poured out into a flat dish to harden. Her mother carefully marked it off in squares before it was too hard to cut easily.

Mrs. Adams's hands were rarely idle. While she taught the children, or listened to John Quincy read, her fingers were flying with the knitting needles. Her maids knit, too, for the stockings worn by the family were made by the fingers of the women in the home. There were many pairs of mittens and gloves to be knit also, for in New England everyone wore them to keep from getting "frost bitten" fingers.

Little girls will want to know how Abby dressed long ago. She wore dresses like her mother, with long full skirts over big hoops. These skirts came almost to her ankles. She usually wore a ruffled apron and sometimes this had a bib. Her shoes were heavy and warm. In the winter she did not wear a hat. She wore a pumpkin

John Quincy and Abby Adams

hood. This was made of heavy material, quilted. It came far down over her face to keep off the cold frosty air.

Perhaps the boys will want to know how John Quincy dressed. He wore clothing like his father. He had waistcoats or vests and wore knee breeches. His coat was made of the same cloth as was his father's. This was trimmed with buttons.

One day John Quincy ran into the house shouting, "Here is a letter from papa. It just came by the post." Mrs. Adams eagerly opened the letter and read:

"Papa and his party made several short stops. They needed rest on their long journey."

" 'New York is a curiosity,' writes papa. But he does not seem to like the new church there as well as he does our own at home."

John Quincy was determined now, he would try to write to his father. He, too, would send a letter by the post. Fortunately his letter has been saved for us.

"Sir——I have been trying ever since you went away to learn to write you a letter. I shall make poor work of it; but, Sir, mama says you will accept my endeavor and that duty to you may be expressed in poor writing as well as good. I hope I grow a better boy, and that you will have no occasion to be ashamed of me when you return. Mr. Thaxter says I learn my books well. I read my books to mama. We all long to see you. I am, Sir, your dutiful son,

JOHN QUINCY ADAMS."

JOHN ADAMS AND HIS COUSIN SAMUEL ADAMS ARRIVE AT A TAVERN IN PHILADELPHIA TO MEET DELEGATES FROM OTHER COLONIES AND TALK OVER THEIR TROUBLES WITH ENGLAND

One day John Quincy said, "Mama, when you read us papa's last letter, he wrote of dining with all the gentlemen of Virginia. Then, he wrote of feasting with Mr. Carroll of Maryland. "Tell me why the men from the other colonies are in Philadelphia."

"Some day soon, I will do so," his mother promised.

The Meeting At Philadelphia

A few days later, Mrs. Adams said, "Come, John Quincy, I will tell you why papa is in Philadelphia while

John Quincy and Abby Adams

I knit this stocking for him. Come, Abby, you can sew your seam and listen to the story too.

"Papa writes that he and Cousin Samuel Adams were met by Dr. Rush of Philadelphia and some other gentlemen who rode out to greet them just outside the city.

"When they reached the city, papa and Cousin Samuel went to the tavern. They had rooms there and invited Dr. Rush and his friends to have supper with them. Listen to papa's letter:

" 'We then rode into the town, dirty, dusty, and tired as we were. We went to the tavern, the most genteel in America. Here we had a fresh welcome and after some time in talk, a curtain was drawn in the other half of the chamber and supper appeared, as elegant as any ever laid upon a table.' "

"Who were the gentlemen, mama?" asked John. "Were they all from Philadelphia?"

"No, indeed," replied Mrs. Adams, "These men were from eleven of the colonies."

"Did they all drive to Philadelphia in a coach as papa and Cousin Samuel did?" asked Abby.

"Oh, no," her mother told her. "The delegates from South Carolina arrived first, papa writes. They were sunburned from their long trip on the packet boat, the "Sea Nymph," which sailed from Charleston. Mr. Washington, Mr. Henry, and Mr. Lee from Virginia rode up on horseback."

"How did the men know when to go to Philadelphia, mama?" asked Abby.

Those Who Dared

"Cousin Samuel has been writing letters to Mr. Henry Lee of Virginia for some time," replied Mrs. Adams. "Cousin Samuel told of the closing of Boston Harbor and other unjust acts of England. The Virginia colony sympathized with us and ordered a day of fasting and prayer. This made the Governor of Virginia angry. He ordered the House of Burgesses to adjourn. They did, but the Virginians met at once in the Raleigh Tavern there in Williamsburg. They decided then to ask all the colonies to send delegates to Philadelphia to discuss their troubles. Philadelphia was chosen for the meeting place because it is about half way between the northern and the southern colonies.

"Papa writes," continued Mrs. Adams, "that all the delegates from the eleven colonies met at the City Tavern and marched to the Carpenters' Hall. This building is as fine as any in the city. There is a large room in it where the meetings are held.

"The men first chose Mr. Pendleton of Virginia to be their president. Cousin Samuel voted that the men should let no religious difference enter into the Continental Congress, as they called their meeting, for some of the men are Puritans, and others are Quakers, Episcopalians, and Catholics. Then the men talked about our troubles here in Massachusetts. Listen to papa's letter. He says, 'The esteem, the affection, the admiration for the people of Boston and Massachusetts were enough to melt a heart of stone. I saw the tears gush into the eyes of the old grave pacific Quakers of Pennsylvania.'

John Quincy and Abby Adams

"Cousin Samuel told how Colonel Washington of Virginia said, 'I will raise a thousand men and support them at my own expense and march at their head for the relief of Boston.'

"The delegates next made a 'Declaration of Rights.' They asked the King to think over the wrongs which had been done to the colonies by taxing them when they did not have any chance to vote in England on the question of whether they should be taxed or not.

"Papa writes that the delegates have become good friends. At first the larger colonies, like Virginia, had more votes than a smaller one. Mr. Patrick Henry of Virginia wanted to keep it that way until he saw how angry it made the smaller colonies. Then he made a great speech and said, 'I am no longer a Virginian. I am an American.' This meant he was willing to give up having more power and do what was best for all."

"Papa must get tired of so much business," sighed Abby as she finished her seam.

"It is not all work, children," replied her mother. "Those stern and staid Quakers are entertaining the delegates often. Listen to papa's account of a day: 'I shall be killed with kindness in this place. We go to Congress at nine and stay until three in the afternoon. Then we dine with some of the nobles of Philadelphia at four o'clock, and feast upon ten thousand delicacies, and then home, fatigued to death with business, company, and care!' "

" 'But the largest entertainment,' writes papa, 'was held

Those Who Dared

at the City Tavern. Over five hundred people were there. They drank many toasts to the King and Queen and to each of their children, the princes and princesses. One toast was like a prayer—that there should be no war between England and her children here in the colonies—that our country should never be stained with the blood of her children.'"

This meeting in Philadelphia lasted for seven long weeks. And Mr. Adams wrote in his diary: "Started for home in a very great rain from the happy, peaceful, elegant, hospitable, and polite city of Philadelphia."

THE LIBRARY

Stories in Other Books

"New Homes for Old," in *These United States and How They Came to Be*, by Gertrude Hartman.

"Colonial Customs," in *Virginia and Virginians*, by Ellie Marcus Marx.

"Master Pormont's School," "School Discipline," "Other Tools of Torture," "Other Schools," in *Ruth of Boston*, by James Otis [Kaler].

"How Our Forefathers Lived in Olden Times," in *Our Nation Begins*, by Eugene C. Barker, William E. Dodd, and Walter P. Webb.

"Plantation Life," in *The Story of Virginia*, by Carrie Hunter Willis and Lucy S. Saunders.

SELF-TESTING GAME

This is a choosing game. Choose the right ending for each sentence. Each correct choice counts 2.

On a piece of paper, number the lines 1 to 10. After each number write the ending that makes the sentence true.

Children of Long Ago

Catalina Schuyler, The Flats, New York

1. Catalina Schuyler liked to visit (the park, the Indian village).
2. The Indian maidens embroidered deer-skin with (wampum beads, bright colored silk).
3. Long ago little girls learned (to be scouts, to cross-stitch samplers).
4. In The Flats, little boys gave their slaves a present of (shoes and a piece of money, switches).

Jack and Patsy Custis, Mount Vernon, Virginia

5. Jack and Patsy Custis loved their stepfather (Colonel Schuyler, George Washington).
6. Patsy went with her mother into the (city, beautiful gardens).
7. Jack Custis loved to (swim, ride and hunt).
8. The packet boat brought presents from (New York, England, Boston).

John Quincy Adams and Abby Adams, Braintree, Massachusetts

9. In the days of John Quincy Adams and Abby Adams, people traveled by (automobile, bus, stage-coach).
10. Girls were taught (to drive cars, to sew and knit).
11. Little girls wore (big hats and short skirts, quilted hoods and long skirts).
12. Boys dressed very much like their fathers in (coats, vests, and knee breeches; sack coats and long pants).

The highest possible score is 24. Count your score.

Choose Something to Do

1. Divide your class into three groups. Each might give a puppet show: one showing the life of Catalina Schuyler at The Flats; one of Jack and Patsy Custis at Mount Vernon;

Those Who Dared

the other of John Quincy Adams and Abby Adams at Braintree.

2. Your class might make soap and dip candles as the people did in early times.

3. You could make a list of the words used in colonial times, but not often heard today.

4. From pictures you have seen, you could draw a sampler, some colonial furniture, a colonial kitchen, and ways of traveling in the early days.

5. On page 94 of this book you will find an exact copy of a sampler made by a little girl of colonial days. Her name was Catharine Chiverton, and the sampler is dated November 14, 1785. See if you can read all the letters and figures on the sampler. Some of them are very old-fashioned.

6. Perhaps your class would enjoy giving a garden party like those given at Mount Vernon in the days of Jack and Patsy Custis. How would the people dress? Of what would they talk? What would they dance?

PART IV

PIONEER LIFE IN THE DAYS OF DANIEL BOONE

CHAPTER XII

A BOY OF THE FRONTIER

"Look, mother," shouted Daniel Boone as he rushed into his log cabin home, "I've a gun! Father gave it to me—a real man's gun!"

"And you deserve it, Daniel," replied his quiet Quaker mother. "Father says you are the best shot for a twelve-year-old boy in this part of Pennsylvania. Now you can prove your gun when we go to the grazing lands."

"When will you go, mother?" asked Daniel.

"I will finish putting the woolen clothes away today," replied his mother. "The blankets are washed, and the cabin is ready for summer. We ought to go tomorrow."

"Good," Daniel cried. "I'll be ready!"

Daniel took long strides as he proudly marched out to the barn with his new gun upon his shoulder. He was a happy boy for two reasons. He had wanted a gun of his own for two long years and now he had one, just like the gun his father carried, and he was going again to take the cows to the grazing lands six miles away.

Daniel liked to go with his mother and stay in the small log cabin for five months, while they tended the cows. There was a cool spring near the tiny cabin and there Mrs. Boone kept the cream sweet and fresh. When the butter was churned, she then patted it into shape before she packed it away in salt for winter.

Those Who Dared

You may think it strange that Daniel could leave home and school so early in the spring. But Daniel Boone's people were frontier folk. They lived far from any neighbors in the wooded lands of Pennsylvania. There were no schools for the children. But Daniel learned quiet gentle manners from his father and mother, who were Quakers. He learned truth and honesty from them, too. Daniel Boone's school was the out-of-doors. He watched the sky before storms and knew which winds brought rains or snows. He knew how to find his way through the forests at night by looking at the stars. He knew how to track wild animals and could shoot them as well as a man. He could call birds to him and could walk through a forest without leaving foot-prints or other signs by which be could be followed.

When Daniel was fourteen his older brother, Samuel, married a Quaker girl, Sarah Day. Sarah liked Daniel and taught him to read and write, but Daniel soon tired of books. He did not like to stay indoors. So he took his gun and spent days at a time in the mountains. There he shot and killed bears, deer, and other animals. He cured the meat for the family and dressed the skins so that he could sell them. When he had enough skins, he carried them to Philadelphia and traded them for lead, hunting knives, and powder.

Daniel tried to help his father, who was a weaver. Mr. Boone's looms were always full of cloth which he made for his family or exchanged with his neighbors for a cow, a horse, or skins. He also had a blacksmith shop

DANIEL BOONE'S FATHER TAKES HIS FAMILY TO NORTH CAROLINA TO LIVE. THEY ARE JOURNEYING ALONG THE "GREAT ROAD" FROM PENNSYLVANIA TO THE YADKIN VALLEY

and Daniel worked there too. Each year Daniel Boone's muscles grew more like iron bands. Each year he spent more time away from home, hunting in the forests, trapping animals, and trading with the friendly Indians.

When Daniel Boone was about sixteen, his father moved to North Carolina. He wanted to live where his cattle could graze for long months in the year. Mr. Boone sold his land and some of his cattle. Then he and his sons built strong wagons and covered them with heavy canvas cloth. The men packed in the few pieces of furniture, the bedclothes, and the clothing. Then the women and children climbed into the wagons and the long journey was begun.

Those Who Dared

The men and boys rode or walked in front and behind to protect the wagons and drive the cattle that would not easily follow. In this way they traveled.

At night they camped near a stream, built a fire, cooked for their meals the game which the hunters of the group had killed. They brought the cattle inside the circle of the wagons and placed men to guard the camp against the Indians. Probably as they sat around the fire they told stories of the adventures of the day. If so, Daniel Boone, as the best hunter of the group, had the greatest adventures to tell. After a long time the Boone party reached their new home in North Carolina. They settled on the Yadkin River under the shadow of the Blue Ridge Mountains. There they found a rich soil, plentiful grazing lands, and game of all kinds.

The men cut down trees and built log cabins which were very much like those they had left in Pennsylvania. They cleared lands for gardens, and soon the Boones felt at home and were happy.

Daniel did his share in the building of the cabin and in helping his father. Then off he went with his gun, shooting bears, wild turkeys, and deer. He met and traded with the Indians, who at first were as friendly as the ones he had known in Pennsylvania.

CHAPTER XIII

DANIEL BOONE GOES TO WAR

The Indians were giving trouble in the far north as well as in the south. The fur trade, as you know, was very rich. Both the English and the French people were trading with the Indians and buying their furs in the valley of the Ohio River. Both nations claimed this land.

England and France finally went to war. England sent General Braddock to America. He brought trained soldiers with a supply of guns and powder.

George Washington was sent from Virginia to help General Braddock. These soldiers from England did not know the ways of the Indians, who fought from behind trees. They did not know the backwoods fighting of the French fur traders. They needed guides to lead them through the dense forest and over mountains. One hundred men from the North Carolina frontier were sent to aid the forces of General Braddock. Among these Daniel Boone was a wagoner and blacksmith.

The English carried their supplies in great heavy wagons which were built for regular roads. They were unfit for the narrow trails or paths which led to the Ohio country, where the English were going to fight the French. The heavy wagons made traveling slow, and this increased the danger from Indian attacks. However, the men traveled many miles before they had any trouble.

Those Who Dared

But when they reached the foot of the mountains in Pennsylvania, they came to a deep ravine, near Turtle Creek.

All at once they were surrounded by Indians, who were led by a French officer. The wagons of supplies were the center of the fight.

Daniel Boone realized his danger. He saw that the English were not able to whip the French and Indians, who outnumbered them. Daniel could save his horses, which he did, by pulling out his sharp knife and cutting the traces that held the horses to the wagon. He then sprang on the back of one and galloped off to safety.

War lasted for several years. Daniel Boone acted as a guide, a scout, and a blacksmith. England won and drove the French from the Ohio country.

During the war Daniel Boone met a man, John Finley, who had been into the Kentucky country. He told Daniel of the rich game, of the fertile valleys, of the tall forests upon the mountains. When Daniel returned to his home in North Carolina, he longed to go adventuring into this western country. He wanted to hunt over those mountains.

CHAPTER XIV

THE BOONES' PIONEER HOME

Daniel Boone, however, was not to go off seeking new hunting grounds just yet. The reason was that he fell in love with a brown-eyed Quaker girl whom he loved too dearly to leave. Daniel Boone and Rebecca Bryan were married, and after a wedding feast they went to live for a short time with Daniel's father and mother. Daniel worked on his cabin, which stood in his father's yard. He stuffed the chinks of the cabin with moss and clay to make it warmer. He chinked the great chimney, which was on the outside of the cabin, with clay and gravel. He coated the inside of it with clay to make it draw better. Daniel cleaned out the huge fireplace and polished the iron crane for his bride. He swung the iron pot ready for Rebecca to cook their simple meals. In that pot would be boiled beans, pork, squash, potatoes, and soups.

Upon the bake-pot on the hearth, Rebecca would put red-hot coals when she wished to broil venison (deer) steak for her hungry hunter. On this bake-pot, Rebecca would also bake brown flour biscuits, corn pone, and cakes.

Of course Rebecca had no silver such as brides have today. She had wooden bowls in which she mixed her bread, and pewter plates, forks, and spoons.

Those Who Dared

The fireplace was an important part of any log cabin. Over it hung the horns of a deer, which held the gun of Daniel Boone. By the side of the fireplace were great bunches of red and green peppers. These were dried and used as seasoning for the dried bacon, venison, and bears' meat which hung around the cabin walls on wooden pegs. On the pegs which did not hold meat were hung the simple clothes of Daniel and Rebecca. In those days, few log cabins had more than one room, with perhaps a dark attic room under the eaves of the roof.

Daniel dressed very much like other pioneer men. He wore a long hunting shirt of homespun cloth. He also had a shirt made of leather which he wore when it was very cold on his hunting trips. His trousers were close-fitting and came to his knees. He wore with these leather leggings or those made from homespun cloth. His shoes were moccasins, like those which the Indians wore, and were made of dressed deer-skin. In the winter, Daniel had to put dried deer's hair in his moccasins to keep his feet warm. This also kept his woolen stockings from getting wet when he waded through streams. Daniel carried a powder horn which swung from the leather belt, in which his hunting knife was fastened.

Daniel's shirt was loose across his chest. He carried in his bosom his food for the day's hunt. It is said that he usually wore a hat instead of the coon-skin cap with its swinging tail which his neighbors wore.

Rebecca's clothing was as simple as her husband's. She wove the cloth for her own homespun dresses and made

DANIEL BOONE BUILDS A CABIN FOR HIS BRIDE

them, too. Her skirts were full and came to her ankles. Her waist fitted snugly and was buttoned up to her neck, which was fitted with a simple collar.

Rebecca Boone was never idle, for when she had finished her cooking, washing, weaving, quilting, and spinning, she still had her knitting to do. She made her own butter and cheese. Soon there were babies to rock to sleep, bathe, and dress.

In the backwoods there were no stores or shops. Each man became expert in some work. Daniel Boone had a blacksmith shop and did smithy work for his neighbors. The miller, in turn, ground Daniel's corn into meal and

Those Who Dared

his wheat into flour, while another neighbor paid Daniel in skins. Each man gave his work in exchange for something which he needed.

Life in the backwoods was simple but it was hard in many ways. There were no doctors, no teachers, and often no minister. The women boiled teas from herbs which they gave to those who had colds and fever. They also made salves for boils and sores and liniments with which they rubbed sprained limbs. The friendly Indians taught the women how to make home remedies.

The children were taught to read, mostly by their mothers, who knew little else besides their a-b-c's and how to add 2 and 2. There were few lawyers and no police. Yet these Quaker backwoods folk were honest men and women, loyal to their families and neighbors, friendly and kind to strangers.

Sometimes a peddler came to the door of a backwoods home. He carried a pack on his back in which were pewter spoons, needles, pins, and trinkets of all kinds. One day a peddler visited the Boone cabin. Rebecca soon learned that he was the friend, John Finley, who had first told her husband about the wonders of the Kentucky country.

"You will stay with us for the winter," Daniel Boone said to his friend when he returned home. And John Finley agreed.

Daniel Boone and his brother listened to Finley's tales of his travels in Kentucky. They longed to hunt the wild bears, turkeys, buffalo, and deer which were found there

The Boones' Pioneer Home

in such large numbers. They began to make plans for a hunting trip. Finley, Daniel Boone, with his brother-in-law, Stuart, and three other neighbors, made up the party. As soon as the men had planted their spring crops they set off.

CHAPTER XV

HUNTING ADVENTURES

Each man rode his own horse and carried his gun, a blanket of bear-skin, a small camp kettle, salt, and powder.

The men rode for thirty days. They followed the hunters' trail. They came to the warriors' path which was worn by Indians as they crossed the mountains.

At last they reached a fine camping site near the Kentucky River. Here the men remained for many months, finding the game as plentiful as John Finley had claimed.

The men needed patience, skill, and steady muscles to be good hunters. They must know how to call the various animals and fowls. They had to know how to change their positions when the wind blew, so that the animals would not scent their enemy, man.

Deer-skins were worth more to the hunters than other things. Each deer-skin was valued at a dollar. The hunters prepared the skins by scraping and drying them. A horse could carry about a hundred deer-skins on his back. The men made straps and harness out of elk-skins for their horse. Buffalo-skins were cured and used for blankets. Beaver-skins were worth more than the deer-skins, but they were not good except in the winter when the fur was thick and glossy.

Daniel Boone and his companions had many dangerous adventures. The Indians surprised and captured

THE WILDERNESS WAS RICH IN GAME FOR HUNTERS AND TRAPPERS

Boone and Stuart. They made the white men tell where their camp was, and then raided it. They took their store of skins and most of their supplies and warned Daniel Boone to stay off the Indian hunting grounds. Frightened by the capture of Stuart and Boone, some of the party returned home.

Just then Squire Boone, who had stayed at home to gather the crop, joined his brother. These two, with Stuart and one other hunter, set up camp for the winter.

One day Stuart did not return. Filled with fear, the other hunter left at once for home. The Boone brothers stayed on and spent the winter in the woods hunting.

In the spring, Squire took the skins to market. Daniel

Those Who Dared

Boone was left "without bread, salt, or sugar," and without the company of even a horse or a dog.

Once he was overtaken by Indians and surrounded. He knew he had to surrender or leap down a steep bank sixty feet below. Without hesitating, Daniel leaped. Fortunately he landed in the top of a small tree. He quickly climbed down and ran along under the bushes. Then he jumped into the stream and crossed to safety.

Daniel's brother after a few months returned from North Carolina. He had sold the skins for good money, and had paid off the family debts. He and Daniel now hunted with vigor. When spring came again, Daniel's brother went to the eastern markets, where he sold for a profit the skins they had taken during the winter. Daniel Boone then returned to his home in North Carolina. He had had two years of adventure in the forest.

CHAPTER XVI

LIFE IN BOONESBORO

The land which is now known as Kentucky was once a fine Indian hunting ground, and the Indians fought each other so fiercely for it that it came to be known as the "dark and bloody ground." A year or two after Boone returned to North Carolina, he and his family, with some other settlers, started to Kentucky, but on the way, near Cumberland Gap, his oldest son was killed by the Indians, and the little party retreated to the Clinch River, where they stayed for about two years while Boone and others were exploring the new country and fighting the Indians.

Then Boone, with thirty strong men, went out to mark a path through the forest and build a fort for others who would follow. The road followed for many miles the trail made by buffaloes. It was named the "Wilderness Road." Boone had been asked to do this by Judge Richard Henderson and some other men who were interested in the western lands.

Boone and his men chose for their settlement a place called Big Lick. Indeed it was a *big lick*. As the party drew near, what a sight greeted their eyes! Hundreds of buffaloes who were licking the salty spot went off through the valley—some running and some walking, with young calves jumping and frolicking by their sides.

BOONESBORO, THE FAMOUS FRONTIER FORT BUILT IN 1775 ON THE KENTUCKY RIVER IN THE "DARK AND BLOODY GROUND" TO PROTECT THE SETTLERS IN KENTUCKY

A fort was begun in April, and in the fall Boone's family with other neighbors came to live in their new home, Boonesboro, named for Daniel Boone.

The fort was much like other pioneer forts. At each corner of the four sides were two-story block houses. Between these the walls were made of posts and the backs of cabins with their roofs sloping inward toward the center of the fort. On these roofs, the men could lie to shoot the savages. The outside walls of the cabins had no windows, but they had port-holes through which the settlers fired upon their enemies. In the sides of the fort

JEMIMA BOONE, BETSY AND FANNY CALLOWAY ARE CAPTURED BY INDIANS

were large gates, through which the cattle were driven inside when Indians came.

The pioneers were in constant danger. One day Jemima, Daniel Boone's fourteen-year-old daughter, went with Betsy and Fanny Calloway to the Kentucky River. They got into a canoe and were paddling on the river. There was a strong current which caught the light canoe and swept it along for a quarter of a mile from the town. The girls were carried to the north side of the river. Imagine their horror when five Indians sprang from the bushes, waded out into the river, and caught hold of their canoe. The girls screamed, but the Indians hurried them along and they were quickly out of sight.

When the girls were missed, Fanny's father, Colonel Calloway, sprang upon his horse. He called for the others to follow him. He hoped to cut off the Indians as they crossed to their towns on the Ohio River.

IN A BLOCKHOUSE AT BOONESBORO FORT DURING AN INDIAN ATTACK. THE WOMEN HELP BY RELOADING THE LONG RIFLES WITH POWDER AND BULLETS AS FAST AS THE GUNS ARE FIRED

Daniel Boone could not wait. He started off on foot with some of his neighbors. Soon he found a trail which the girls had marked by breaking twigs or tearing their clothes along the path, as the Indians carried them off. This trail Boone followed.

Two long anxious days passed before Daniel Boone and his men caught up with the Indians and their prisoners. They tramped thirty-five miles before they found the camp of the cruel savages. Daniel Boone and his

Life in Boonesboro

men made a quick raid and rescued the girls, who were unharmed. Two Indians were killed, and the others escaped into the woods.

Some time later Daniel Boone himself was captured by the Indians and made a member of a tribe. He was adopted by Chief Big Fish as his son and was called Big Turtle.

When Boone learned that these Indians were going to attack Boonesboro, he determined to escape. He watched for his chance. It soon came. A flock of wild turkeys appeared near the camp where the Indians were boiling salt. The Indians began to shoot. Daniel slipped quietly away on swift feet. He traveled day and night, only stopping long enough to eat one meal and to rest.

Daniel Boone reached Boonesboro and told his neighbors of their danger. He urged them to strengthen their forts and to put all four blockhouses in order. Because of this warning, the Indians failed in their attack when they came to surprise the town.

CHAPTER XVII

DANIEL BOONE GOES FARTHER WEST

Daniel Boone was one of the most noted pioneer backwoodsmen. He was fearless, honest, and trustful. Yet he was not a good business man. He failed to have his land claims made legal by a lawyer. When Kentucky was formed, Daniel Boone lost all his land. As the country became more thickly settled, he moved farther west. He said that he wanted "more elbow room."

When Daniel Boone left Kentucky he owed a great deal of money, but in Missouri, his new home, he hunted until he had a large supply of skins. When he sold these, he took the money and went back to Kentucky to pay all his debts. After he did this he had only fifty cents left, but he said he could die happy because he owed no man anything.

In Missouri, when he took up more land, he did not go to the trouble to have proper records made of his lands. So he lost all his land in Missouri, too. He was now an old man. The Congress of the United States heard of his loss. Congress decided the United States owed Daniel Boone a debt, for it was he who had "opened the way for millions of fellow-men," to find homes in the west. The United States made good his land claims.

Daniel Boone lived to be eighty-seven years old. The year before he died, a visitor found him in the ruins of an

Pioneer Life

old blockhouse. He sat before a fire roasting a piece of venison steak on the ramrod of his gun. To the end he enjoyed the pioneer life he had always known. He was a man respected and beloved by a large family and by the settlers whom he had helped to "go west."

THE LIBRARY
Stories in Other Books

"Hunters, Daniel Boone," "Blockhouses and Forts," in *Stories of Pioneer Life for Young Readers,* by Florence Bass.

"The Musket Telegraph," in *Stories of American Life and Adventure,* by Edward Eggleston.

"Daniel Boone and His Grapevine Swing," in *Stories of Great Americans for Little Americans,* by Edward Eggleston.

"Daniel Boone Leads the Way to Kentucky," in *Our Nation Begins,* by Eugene C. Barker, William E. Dodd, and Walter P. Webb.

"Daniel Boone," in *Makers of Our Nation,* by Reuben Post Halleck, and Juliette Frantz.

"Pioneer Life," in *Virginia and Virginians,* by Ellie Marcus Marx.

"Pioneer Days," in *The Story of Virginia,* by Carrie Hunter Willis and Lucy S. Saunders.

SELF-TESTING GAME

This is a word game. On a sheet of paper, write this short story of Daniel Boone, putting in the missing words.

When a small boy, Daniel Boone spent the summer with his mother in a cabin and tended the ——. He always liked to ——. He helped his father —— and worked in the —— shop. In the war he was a —— and ——. There he met his friend —— ——. These two men, with others, went

Those Who Dared

to ———. There Daniel Boone hunted for ——— years. Later he and about thirty other men opened the ——— ——— and built the fort of ——— ———. Then Daniel Boone took ——— ——— to live in Kentucky. When Kentucky was more thickly settled, Daniel Boone moved to ———.

Choose Something to Do

1. Draw scenes in the life of Daniel Boone. Take the best scenes drawn by your class and make a moving picture which will tell the story of Daniel Boone.
2. Perhaps some of the class would like to build the fort of Boonesboro.
3. Find another pioneer story and tell it to the class.
4. Write a paragraph telling how you think a pioneer girl might spend a day; a pioneer boy.
5. Find the "Boone Trail" on a highway map, and see how closely it follows the life and adventures of Daniel Boone.

PART V

THE COLONIES COME TOGETHER

CHAPTER XVIII

THE COLONISTS WANT TO BE FREE

"British Soldiers March Into Lexington! Minute Men Refuse to Disband! Eight Minute Men Killed and Several Wounded! Citizens of Concord Searched for Guns and Ammunition!"

This was the serious news which greeted the delegates from the colonies in May, 1775, when they met in Philadelphia for the Second Continental Congress. It cast a gloom over the whole city, for now England had taken the lives of some of her colonists. War could not be far away!

The delegates were solemn as they took their seats in the chamber. John Hancock presided over the meeting, and it opened with prayer.

Once more John and Samuel Adams, Patrick Henry, and others talked over what was best to be done. Richard Henry Lee and Samuel Adams wanted to declare war. Colonel Washington said little, but in his full uniform he looked ready for war, and war was surely coming.

The convention must choose a commander for the army of soldiers who had already gone to Boston as soon as they had heard the news. John and Samuel Adams, and the others voted for Colonel Washington to be in command of all the American soldiers. They knew he had been a scout in the Ohio country as well as a soldier.

THE OPENING PRAYER OF THE SECOND CONTINENTAL CONGRESS IN PHILADELPHIA, IN MAY, 1775, AFTER THE BATTLE OF LEXINGTON

He was more suited to command the army than any other person in all the colonies. Washington left the Congress at once and rode to Cambridge, where, under an elm tree, he took command.

Washington's plan was to draw his soldiers in a ring around the British until they were surrounded. This he did, and forced them to get on their ships and sail away. He felt sure that they were going to New York.

Everywhere the colonists were talking frankly to each other, and beginning to feel that they must work together

The Colonists Want Freedom

for their new country. "I am no longer a Virginian," said Patrick Henry. "I am an American!" Others were impatient and wished that Congress would tell the King they were not going to be English subjects any longer. Everyone now wanted "independence," as they called freedom from England.

There were a few families who were still loyal to the King and hoped that war would not come. They soon were called Loyalists, or Tories. These were not popular with the other colonists and many of them left America and went to Canada. A year passed. All the colonies were in favor of separating from England.

One of the youngest men in the Congress was a young man, tall and sandy-haired, with twinkling blue eyes. His name was Thomas Jefferson, and he was a delegate from Virginia. He heard Richard Henry Lee say that the colonies had a right to be free. His eyes burned with excitement when Mr. Lee spoke: "These United Colonies are, and of right ought to be free and independent states!" He also said the colonists should no longer be loyal to the King and that all ties should be cut. This was a "Declaration." The delegates decided to write such a paper and send it to the people and to the King.

This Declaration must be carefully worded and very carefully written. A committee of five delegates was chosen and the young delegate, Thomas Jefferson of Virginia, was chairman of it.

The members of his committee knew that he had studied law at William and Mary College and that he

Those Who Dared

was a great writer as well. They asked him to write the Declaration of Independence!

Thomas Jefferson went to his rooms in the home of a bricklayer and shut himself up in the little parlor. There he wrote and tore up sheet after sheet of paper. He worked day and night for eighteen days. It is said when he could not write because his hand was cramping, he would get his fiddle and play until he was rested again. At last he finished the Declaration of Independence.

Jefferson read this to the Congress on the first of July. What a stir it caused! Some of the peace-loving delegates thought it was too strong against England. These men argued and debated. Others were just as determined to keep it as it had been written.

Young Thomas Jefferson sat for three days during these debates. His fair cheeks flushed as he heard the men argue against it. He was embarrassed when others praised it, but he himself never spoke a word. At last the votes were taken and the Declaration was passed.

Of course each colony had to vote on so important a question. Delaware could not cast her vote, because one of her three delegates, Mr. Rodney, was absent. The two others were divided. One was for adopting the Declaration and one was against it. Mr. Rodney was needed to break the tie.

"Where is Mr. Rodney?" asked a member. "Delaware needs him. I am sure he is for the Declaration!"

Mr. McKean, the delegate who favored the Declaration, spoke. "I know where he is. I will send for him."

"THE CONGRESS IS MET; THE DEBATE'S BEGUN, AND LIBERTY LAGS FOR THE VOTE OF ONE, WHEN INTO THE HALL, NOT A MOMENT LATE, WALKS CAESAR RODNEY, THE DELEGATE"

Now Mr. Rodney was at his home in Delaware, eighty miles away. Mr. McKean called a messenger and sent him off to Mr. Rodney's home, "Tell him he must come at once," said Mr. McKean. "We cannot afford to lose a moment."

The messenger rode all night. He rode into the yard while Mr. Rodney was having his breakfast. He went in hurriedly and told Mr. Rodney his errand.

"Have my fastest riding horse saddled," cried Mr. Rodney. He rode off at a gallop, and when that horse was tired, he stopped along the way and hired another. All day the delegates awaited impatiently to see if he had

Those Who Dared

arrived. The afternoon passed. Evening came. Still Mr. Rodney had not come.

Then, tired, spattered with mud and dust, Mr. Rodney rushed up the steps of Carpenters' Hall and cast the vote which swung Delaware into line and made the Declaration of Independence possible.

Now each man had to sign his name to the paper, or document as the lawyers called it. These delegates realized that "England considered it as treason, the penalty for which is death." Yet they risked their lives and fortunes for what they considered right.

John Hancock signed his name first. As he wrote in large bold letters he said, "John Bull won't need spectacles to read that."

Another joked too, "Now we will all hang together!" Benjamin Franklin replied as he signed, "If we do not hang together, we shall all hang separately!"

On the Fourth of July there was a holiday in Philadelphia. A long line of delegates formed and marched through the state house grounds to the platform which was built there. John Hancock went up the steps first, followed by Benjamin Franklin, Richard Henry Lee, John Adams, and others, and towering above them was the tall, slender Thomas Jefferson, the writer of the Declaration which was about to be read!

John Nixon, who had a clear ringing voice, was asked to read the Declaration. A hush fell over the crowd as he read. Then a great shout arose. Hands were clapped while guns were fired. Bells rang to show how pleased

The Colonists Want Freedom

the people were over declaring their freedom from England! The rest of the day was spent in rejoicing over the Declaration of Independence. When night came, a bonfire was lighted which threw the glow of freedom to the far-away country side. This was our first Fourth of July celebration.

Copies of the famous Declaration were sent by fast riders to all the colonies. Everywhere it was joyfully received, with the firing of cannon and with dinners and bonfires.

CHAPTER XIX

THE SPIRIT OF THE PEOPLE

For more than one hundred and fifty years, the colonists had lived as pioneers. They had often saved their lives by fighting the Indians. They had made their living by clearing the lands and by hunting and fishing. They had endured with courage the hardships of life in a new land. They had always loved home and country. Now, to the love of home and country, was added a greater love of freedom and the strength and bravery to win it.

Many stories have come to us which show the spirit of these people who could not be conquered.

Loyal to Country

When England saw that the colonists were determined to fight for their freedom, she tried to get some leaders to bring about friendly feelings toward the mother country. These leaders offered General Reed of Pennsylvania a large sum of money and honors if he would help to bring about this friendly understanding. "I am not worth purchasing," said the honest and loyal man, "but such as I am the King of England is not rich enough to buy me."

Major Molly

Women, too, showed the same spirit of loyalty and courage.

The British army was on its way to New York. Wash-

"THE DAY WAS OURS, AND THE SINKING SUN
LOOKED DOWN ON THE FIELD OF MONMOUTH WON,
AND MOLLY STANDING BESIDE HER GUN"

ington followed. The two armies met in battle. Soldiers were firing the American cannons. It was a terribly hot day in June, and the soldiers suffered from thirst. Molly Hays, the wife of one of the men, brought water to the field of battle. When she came with her pitcher of water, the soldiers would cry out, "Hurrah for Molly Pitcher!"

But Molly Pitcher could do more than bring water. She was a strong brave woman. When her husband was overcome by the heat, quickly she took his place, loaded the cannon, and fired. There she stood doing her husband's work while the battle lasted.

FRANCIS MARION, THE SWAMP FOX, OF SOUTH CAROLINA, EXTENDS HOSPITALITY TO A BRITISH OFFICER

The men now called her "Major Molly," and General Washington honored her for her bravery and courage.

FRANCIS MARION, THE SWAMP FOX

In the swamps of the Carolinas, brave colonists, too few in number to attack the enemy openly, fought for the cause of freedom. Among those in South Carolina was a band of soldiers known as "Marion's Men." Like Robin Hood and his followers, they met in the woods.

The Spirit of the People

They would dart out, strike the enemy, take prisoners, and flee before they could be caught.

One day a British officer was sent to arrange an exchange of prisoners. He was blindfolded and brought into Marion's camp in the dense woods. When the bandage was taken from his eyes, he saw poorly dressed men sleeping on the ground without cover or tents. The mild and gentle Marion, who received him so courteously, he could hardly believe to be the so-called "Swamp Fox," who had caused so much trouble.

Marion invited his visitor to dinner. When the meal was brought, there was nothing but potatoes served on pieces of bark.

The officer was surprised and said, "Surely you have something besides potatoes. Your men do not live on as little food as this."

"Yes," replied Marion, "only today, as we have a guest, there are more potatoes than usual."

The officer returned to his army and said, "Such men as these cannot be conquered."

CHAPTER XX

BENJAMIN FRANKLIN, OUR MESSENGER TO FRANCE

When the strain of war was pressing heavily upon the colonies, Congress decided to send a committee of men to France, hoping that they might get help for our country.

France had for a long time been an enemy of England. Now, in the struggle that England was having with her colonies, France really wished to help the colonists, but she feared to come openly to their relief because she would be in a bad position if England won.

Congress knew this. So it looked around for men who could make France believe that the colonies would, in the end, be victors. Benjamin Franklin was among those chosen. Although Franklin was seventy years old, Congress could not have made a wiser choice. Franklin had spent many years abroad. He was well known and highly honored. Best of all he was very much liked. He was full of wit and humor. If things looked dark and gloomy, he could in a few words describe the situation, and the people would smile.

When he was asked to go to France he said, "I am old and good for nothing, but as the storekeepers say about their remnant of cloth, 'I am but a fag end, and you may have me for what you please.'"

BENJAMIN FRANKLIN'S PRINTING PRESS. FRANKLIN WAS TWELVE YEARS OLD WHEN HE BEGAN TO LEARN THE PRINTING TRADE

Franklin's Stories

Not only did the French government listen to Franklin, but the French people enjoyed his fun and his stories, of which he had many. Perhaps he told some of his French friends of the time when he was a little boy and was given some coppers, or pennies. Away he ran to the toy-shop and bought a whistle. The grown people in the

Those Who Dared

house were so much annoyed with the noise he made, that they asked, "How much did you pay for your whistle?"

He replied, "All my pennies."

Then they laughed and told him what else he might have bought for his money. "You paid too dear for your whistle," they said.

Franklin never forgot. "Always afterward in life," he said, "I watched to see I did not pay too dear for my whistle."

As a little boy he noticed everything. He saw the trade of Boston, the carpenters at work, the masons building walls.

One day little Benjamin was fishing with some boys. Their feet sank in the muddy ground. Benjamin looked up and saw some stones where workmen had been building.

Then he said to the boys, "There, don't you see?"

They didn't understand because they didn't notice like Benjamin.

"Don't you see?" said he. "We can make a wharf out of those stones. Then we will not be bothered by this mud."

At once work was started and Benjamin had the joy of seeing his ideas carried out. The wharf was finished.

The next day when the workmen returned, they had something to say about their stones being moved. The pleasure of the boys was turned to pain. But Benjamin had showed that he was a leader. He had begun to do things.

BENJAMIN FRANKLIN'S EXPERIMENT WITH A KITE PROVED THAT LIGHTNING IS ELECTRICITY

Franklin Draws Electricity from the Clouds

Franklin was the first in this country to draw electricity from the clouds. One day, with his son he went out into a field during a storm. There with a kite, made of thin silk handkerchiefs stretched over a cedar frame and with a long cord and a key attached, he showed that lightning was electricity. He therefore made lightning rods to draw electricity safely to the ground.

He had great curiosity and was always trying to find out something. In England, he was honored because of

Those Who Dared

his knowledge and because he had done many important things.

Not only could Franklin entertain his friends by his stories and witty sayings, but he could write books and articles as well.

He owned a newspaper in Philadelphia. Many people read this because it was full of fun. In England and America his *Poor Richard's Almanack* is quoted even today.

The people in France knew his writings. They knew of his work in electricity, and they soon knew and loved him.

When he talked with men in France about the affairs of the United States, he was wise and calm, and he noticed everything, as he had done when he was a boy. When news came that the armies of the colonists were losing, he quietly and wisely said, "It will turn out all right." Finally, France agreed with him. She recognized the United States as a free country and was willing to lend money and send men and ships to her relief.

Franklin Before the King and Queen

Franklin and his committee were presented to the King and Queen of France. Other members of the committee appeared in court dress with wig and sword, but Franklin, in order to be like himself, must be different. He appeared dressed in plain but rich brown velvet with ruffles in the front and at the wrist, and with white stockings and silver buckles.

Benjamin Franklin

Later Mr. Deane returned home. Franklin remained. Mr. John Adams came over to take Mr. Deane's place. Mr. Adams, a serious, orderly, business-like man, could not understand Franklin's popularity.

His picture was everywhere. His figure was copied in busts and pictures of his face were placed in jewelry. He wrote his daughter that his face was as well known in France as the face of the Man in the Moon.

At last Franklin, who understood the French and whom the the French could understand, was given sole charge of the business for the United States government in that country. France helped the United States not only by loans but even by gifts.

Franklin was now seventy-eight years old. He wanted to go home. He had for eight years been our messenger in France. Congress sent Thomas Jefferson to succeed him. When Jefferson reached France, someone asked, "Is it you, who replaced Dr. Franklin?" Jefferson replied, "I am only his successor, sir; no one can replace him."

CHAPTER XXI

THE HERO OF THE NORTHWEST

"Halt! Who goes there?" called an English guard at Fort Kaskaskia. It was a warm night in July. Two American scouts in the darkness without, scarcely breathed.

The only sound the listening guard heard was the music of the fiddles which floated out from the dance hall within the fort. His thoughts turned to the dance hall, and he marched toward the twinkling lights.

What a merry scene flashed before the windows! Bright candle-light showed the faces of pretty girls, dressed in tight waists with soft lace at their throats. Their long full skirts swept gracefully to the music. They made a pretty picture, as they danced with the English officers and soldiers in their red coats.

The two American scouts stole away in the darkness, as silently as Indians, to report to Colonel George Rogers Clark near the Kaskaskia River.

"All is quiet, Colonel Clark," reported the scouts, "except for a dance within the fort."

"Good," replied Clark. He spoke to an officer and the order, "Forward March!" was given. And off marched the little band of American soldiers on their big adventure—to capture the most important English fort in the West.

Hero of the Northwest

When Clark and his men reached Kaskaskia River, it was midnight. He ordered his men to capture the ferryman who took the men and their supplies across the river. Little did the ferryman know then of the brave American soldier, George Rogers Clark.

Years before our story begins, a tall red-headed Virginian named George Rogers Clark left his home. He was only nineteen then. He became a pioneer in Kentucky. There he learned to be a scout, a hunter, and a fighter. He was with Daniel Boone and helped to survey thousands of acres of land in the Bloody Ground. He also helped Daniel Boone fight the Indians in their attacks against the settlers. Once Clark walked most of the seven hundred miles back to Virginia to get powder and bullets from Governor Patrick Henry when the settlers in Kentucky faced death from Indian attacks and had little powder left for their defense.

Now Clark was doing his part in the Revolutionary War. You remember that the French had trading posts and forts along the Ohio and Mississippi rivers. As you know, the English took these when they drove the French out of the Ohio country. Now the English officers at these forts were giving the Americans much trouble. They were getting the Indians to fight for the English against the Americans. The Indian raids on the backwoods settlers and pioneers kept many men at home to protect their families. They could not join the army in the war against England.

George Rogers Clark had a plan. If he could capture

Those Who Dared

these English forts, then the officers could not arouse the Indians against the settlers, and the settlers could make peace with the Indians. Besides this, Clark knew that the land on which the English forts were located was very rich. He wanted this land to belong to America instead of to England.

But he had to get permission from the governor of Virginia first, because this country was a part of the colony of Virginia. So Clark traveled hundreds of miles to talk his plan over with his old friend, Patrick Henry, the governor of Virginia.

"How many men will you need, Clark?" asked Governor Henry. "We can ill afford to spare a man from Virginia just at this time."

"I should have five hundred," replied Clark. "But I will get my own soldiers, Governor Henry, if you will give me a commission. Get the Assembly of Virginia to order my supplies and have them sent to Pittsburgh."

Governor Henry approved Clark's plan and so did the Virginia Assembly. Clark was given his commission and the supplies were sent to Pittsburgh.

But Clark had a hard time getting even one hundred and fifty men. He built a boat at Pittsburgh on which to float his supplies down the Ohio River. When he reached the falls of the Ohio his men pitched camp. Other men from Kentucky and Pennsylvania joined his little band.

Now Clark told his men, for the first time, that he was going to fight the English. Some of them turned back

Hero of the Northwest

when Clark told them his plans. But one hundred and seventy-five men loved their leader, Colonel Clark. These men with Clark went down the river in boats until they came to the Tennessee River. In southern Illinois they tied their canoes in the tall reeds where no one could find them. They had no horses or wagons; so they had to carry their supplies in packs on their backs. How their muscles ached as they marched through those lowlands and stumbled through the swampy places near the rivers! They came at last to the level country. This they knew to be English territory. They now marched at night to keep from being seen by the enemy. At last their long march was over! Kaskaskia was before them!

When Clark and his men entered Kaskaskia, they found only a guard or two, and these they placed under arrest. Clark went into the fort where the dance was being held. He opened the door and stood looking on at the gay scene. An Indian near by looked at him closely and recognized him. He gave a terrific war-whoop and told the English officers who Clark was.

"Keep on dancing, but now you are dancing under the American flag!" Clark said.

The next day he called together the people of Kaskaskia, who were mostly French. He quickly told them they had nothing to fear from his soldiers. He wanted them to promise they would be faithful to the American cause. This the people were glad to do. Clark also explained to them why his country was at war with England. He told them that France was helping the Ameri-

GEORGE ROGERS CLARK AT KASKASKIA

cans in their war for freedom. The people of Kaskaskia had never really cared for the British rule. Now they were not sorry to see the English flag come down and the American flag wave over the fort at Kaskaskia!

THE CAPTURE OF VINCENNES

When General Hamilton, the commander of the English at Detroit, heard of Clark's success, he decided to

Hero of the Northwest

stop him. So he took some English troops and Indians and started out to drive Clark out of the Illinois country. First he captured the French village of Vincennes, and its fort. Then he decided to stay there for a while because the whole country was flooded and the weather was bitterly cold. Clark said, "I must take Hamilton or he will take me." He would seize the English in the dead of winter.

Clark and his men built a large boat. He placed his cannon in charge of forty of his best picked men and sent them to the Wabash River.

"Meet me at Vincennes," ordered Clark. He told these men his plans. He and the others would take the long march overland.

What a long tiresome journey that was! Clark kept his men encouraged by his songs and jokes. He shared his food with his hungry men. He shared his blankets, too. When they came to the marshy lowlands, the winter rains had set in. The ground was thawing, and they slipped about in the black mud. The streams were all swollen, and they had to cut trees in order to float across the rivers. For days the men could not find a place to make a fire. They could not dry their wet clothing. Many of the men had colds. They had little food. They were weak from hunger. The men marched in water up to their breasts. They laughed at the little drummer who beat his drum merrily sitting on the shoulders of a tall sergeant.

When they came to the Wabash, they made camp.

THROUGH THE FLOODED LOWLANDS TO VINCENNES

While they were talking, a French trapper came into camp.

"Will you take a letter to your people in Vincennes?" asked Clark. The man agreed and Clark wrote, asking the people of Vincennes to stay indoors that night, as he was planning to attack the English fort.

"Post this letter in the town where all your people can read it," Clark told the trapper.

That night the Americans entered Vincennes. There they found that the people had read the letter, but no one

Hero of the Northwest

had carried the news of the planned attack to the English within the fort. The friendly people of Vincennes even gave Clark and his men some powder and bullets.

"Bang! Bang! Bang! Bang!" roared Clark's guns.

"Man the cannon at the port-holes," ordered Hamilton, and his English soldiers ran to obey.

"Aim at the port-holes, men," ordered Clark. But his men needed no such order. They were already shooting. Those backwoods men were crack shots. They picked off the English soldiers at the port-holes. For twenty-four hours the heavy fire kept up. Hamilton realized he could not defeat the determined Clark. He asked for terms. Clark refused to give any except that Hamilton surrender the fort. His soldiers, he said, were very angry at the stories of the outrages which the English encouraged the Indians to carry on against the settlers. However, he granted very easy terms, and the American flag floated over Vincennes.

Clark and his men held these forts in Indiana and Illinois. All of this rich territory now belonged to America, and thus the Mississippi River became the western boundary of the new nation. If it had not been for General Clark's daring plan, think what America might have lost!

Clark was given eight thousand acres of land in what is now Indiana for his services. His soldiers were also paid in land for their work.

The way to the West, through Pittsburgh, was now open. Settlers had nothing to stop them from going into the rich lands of the Mississippi and Ohio river valleys.

CHAPTER XXII

FREEDOM IS WON WITH THE HELP OF FRIENDS FROM OVER THE SEA

Although for a long time France feared to come openly to help the colonies in their struggles, this was not so with Lafayette, who belonged to a family highly honored in France. He was just nineteen years old. He had wealth, a beautiful home, and a lovely young wife. Yet he was willing to leave all these to fight for freedom, even the freedom of a strange land.

Against the wishes of his king, his family, and friends, he engaged a ship at his own expense and with a few other officers set sail for America.

He landed in South Carolina where he was heartily welcomed. At once he gave of his own funds to furnish near-by soldiers with clothing and supplies. Then he started for Philadelphia to appear before Congress.

Between the towns and villages of the colonies there were large tracts of unsettled land. Through these there were not even stage-coach roads. Lafayette made the trip to Philadelphia on horseback. This took more than a month. There Congress received him as joyfully as the colonists in South Carolina. He was made major-general, for which he received no pay. He asked only to serve.

As a member of Washington's staff, the young, fearless, and lovable Lafayette became a great favorite of the

Freedom Is Won

older general. A few months afterwards, when Lafayette was wounded, General Washington said to the doctor, "Care for him as if he were my son."

The next year after Lafayette came to America, France decided to come to help us. Later, Lafayette returned to his home country to give advice about ships and soldiers to be sent over for service. Not long after he came back to America, he was given charge of an army in Virginia. His soldiers were devoted to him. They were a small force, and were too few to stop the heartless Benedict Arnold, who destroyed much property and caused suffering in Virginia. Lafayette's men became discouraged. Some of them deserted. General Lafayette made his army see how wrong such conduct was. Then he offered to let any man who wished to, go home. Not one accepted, nor did any others desert. They chose to follow their general. The story is told that one man who was not able to walk, hired a cart that he might keep up with his comrades.

Soon after this time Cornwallis, one of the greatest generals in the English army, came into Virginia. He was amused at the thought of Lafayette, twenty-three years old, fighting him. He said "The boy cannot escape me," but Cornwallis had something to learn. Lafayette, as a leader, was not a boy. With an army one-fourth the size of that of Cornwallis, he held the English general in check.

Another English general, Clinton, in New York, feared Washington and his men. Clinton told Cornwallis

THE SURRENDER OF CORNWALLIS AT YORKTOWN, OCTOBER 19, 1781

to stay near the coast in Virginia so that his army could come to help Clinton in New York if George Washington attacked him.

Caught In a Trap

Now Lafayette helped Washington lay a trap with the French and American forces to catch Cornwallis and his army.

Freedom Is Won

Cornwallis went to Yorktown, where he and his officers stationed themselves in the fine old home of Governor Nelson. Before Clinton heard of it, Washington had stolen away from New York and was far on his way to Virginia to join his forces with Lafayette's against Cornwallis.

The French fleet closed the Virginia water-way and so trapped Cornwallis. He could not escape. He was "bottled up" at Yorktown.

Governor Nelson, by his own orders, directed the soldiers to fire their cannons on his lovely home, which sheltered Cornwallis and his staff. Today some of these cannon balls may be seen in the walls of the Nelson house. There was no escape from the patriotism of the Americans and from the trap in which the English army had been caught. On October 19, 1781, Cornwallis surrendered. Our friends from over the sea had helped our country to gain freedom.

CHAPTER XXIII

A PLAN TO LIVE BY: THE CONSTITUTION

More than two years after Cornwallis surrendered, Washington said good-bye to his army in New York. With tears in his eyes, he embraced each officer and then left for home, reaching Mount Vernon on Christmas Eve. After eight years of absence, what a pleasure it must have been to be once more at his beloved home.

But he was not allowed to remain long. His country needed him and, as before, he answered the call of duty.

The thirteen sister states, colonies no longer, now that they were free, had to make some plan by which they could work and live together like a large family. Men as delegates from each colony met again in Philadelphia. Washington, because he was so much loved, was made the president of the group, or convention as it was called. Benjamin Franklin, now a very old man, was there. Alexander Hamilton, a bright young man very close to Washington, came with what he thought were fine ideas for the sister states. But James Madison of Virginia had the best ideas of all.

For four months the delegates worked together trying to decide what would be for the good of all. This was not easy to do. The sister states acted as real sisters sometimes do. They were selfish and many times thought chiefly of themselves.

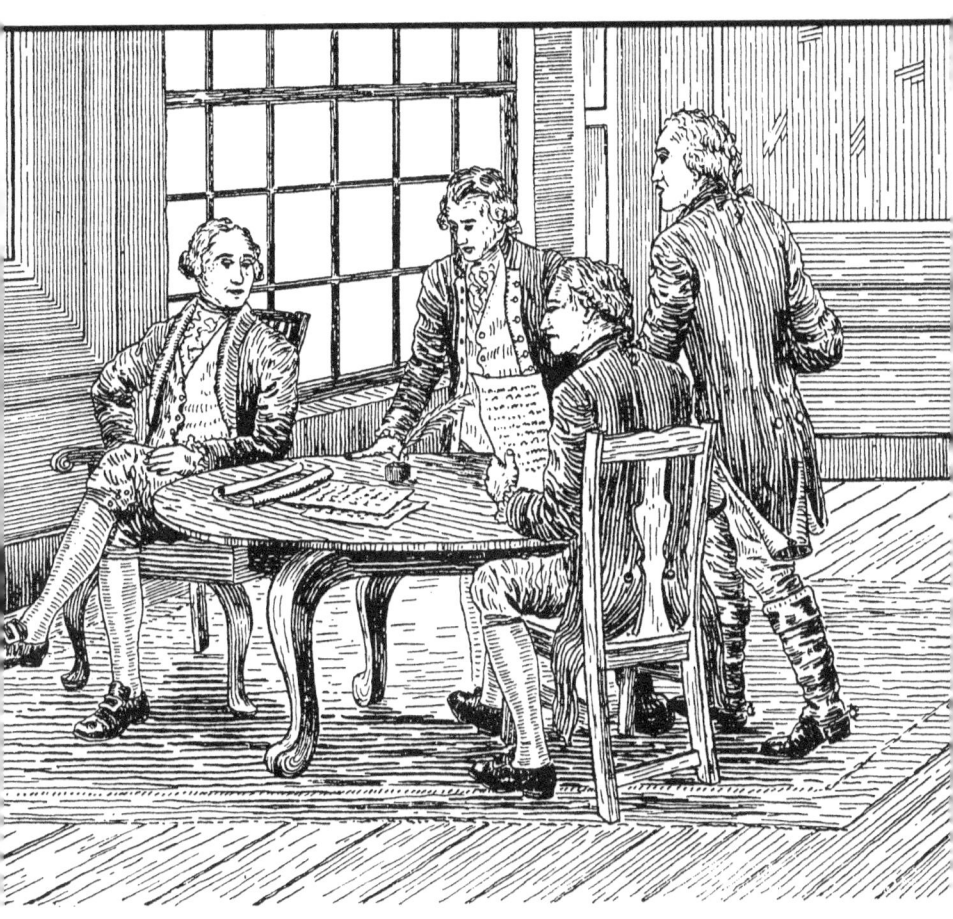

A COMMITTEE WORKING ON THE CONSTITUTION OF THE UNITED STATES. IT TOOK FOUR MONTHS TO COMPLETE THIS FAMOUS DOCUMENT. IT WAS SIGNED BY THIRTY-NINE MEMBERS OF THE CONVENTION

The delegates did not tell the newspapers what they were thinking and saying. They worked behind closed doors, and no reporter was allowed to enter. Even today we would know little of that convention had not Mr. Madison kept a careful record of what was said and done. No wonder he was called "The Father of the Constitution." The "Constitution" is the name of this plan of working and living together.

Finally, the Constitution was made. It was a paper

Those Who Dared

not longer than twelve or fifteen pages. Yet next to the Declaration of Independence, it is the most important paper ever written in our country. Now the states had to decide whether they would accept this plan of government.

Alexander Hamilton did a very noble thing. His plan of union was very different from the one agreed upon in the convention. Yet when the Constitution was made, he did everything in his power to get his state, New York, to accept it. In this and in other ways he served his country well.

At last all the thirteen sister states accepted the Constitution as the plan by which they would work and live. When you are older you will read more about this. The Constitution said that there should be a president of the United States. George Washington was chosen as the first president.

THE LIBRARY

Stories in Other Books

"The Birth of a Nation," in *These United States and How They Came to Be*, by Gertrude Hartman.

"Patrick Henry: The Voice of the Revolution," "A Friend from France," "Building the Ship of State," in *The Story of Virginia*, by Carrie Hunter Willis and Lucy S. Saunders.

"General Washington Commands the American Army," in *Our Nation Begins*, by Eugene C. Barker, William E. Dodd, and Walter P. Webb.

"Washington as a General in the Revolution," *Virginia and Her Builders*, by Mabel Flick Altstetter and Richard Lee Morton.

The Colonies Come Together

'Francis Marion, the Swamp Will o' the Wisp," "Lafayette, the Servant of Mankind," in *Makers of the Nation*, by Fanny E. Coe.

"How Franklin Found Out Things," "Franklin Asks the Sunshine Something," "Franklin and the Kite," "Franklin's Whistle," "Marion's Tower," "Clark and His Men," in *Stories of Great Americans for Little Americans*, by Edward Eggleston.

"Benjamin Franklin," in *Makers of Our Nation*, by Reuben Post Halleck and Juliette Frantz.

"Making a Government for the New Nation," in *Our Nation Grows Up*, by Eugene C. Barker.

Self-Testing Game

This is another matching game. Match the words in Column II with the names in Column I to which they belong. Each name correctly matched counts 3.

I	II
1. Thomas Jefferson	1. "John Bull won't need spectacles to read that."
2. John Hancock	2. Surrended Yorktown, 1781
3. Francis Marion	3. Declaration of Independence
4. Benjamin Franklin	4. Commander of American army
5. Lafayette	5. "Swamp Fox"
6. Cornwallis	6. Messenger, or minister to France
7. George Washington	7. Hero of the Northwest
8. George Rogers Clark	8. Friend from France

The highest possible score is 24. What is your score?

Choose Something to Do

1. If there are places in your community connected with colonial days, your class or a group of your classmates might visit these and report the interesting things that you see.

Those Who Dared

2. Make a travelogue showing places and events during this period when the settlers were planning and fighting to become a new nation. As the picture is shown, one of your group may be behind the scene and tell of the event.

3. Let different members of your class take the part of someone who helped to form the new nation. In a few sentences, let the person introduce himself without giving the name. Then see if others can guess who is being represented.

4. Construct a floor scene showing the surrender of the British at Yorktown.

5. You might find out if there are people in your community whose forefathers fought for the freedom of their country from England.

PART VI

OUR COUNTRY–A NEW NATION

CHAPTER XXIV

A LITTLE GIRL CROWNS A PRESIDENT

Angelica Peale was an impatient little girl one April day, long ago in 1789. She awoke early in her Philadelphia home. She was dressed in her new white dress with a tight waist and full skirt. Her hair was parted, curled, and held in place by a broad band of ribbon. There were spring flowers in water, waiting for her. Today all her friends, too, were dressed in white and were going to strew the highway with flowers as General Washington passed through on his way to New York.

"Now, Angelica, be patient," urged Mrs. Peale. "General Washington will be late. The riders have just returned to tell the townspeople that it will be hours before he arrives."

"Why, Mother," Angelica protested, "I thought all soldiers were prompt, especially the great General Washington."

"General Washington is a prompt man, as we know," replied her mother, "but he makes slow progress as he journeys to New York to become our first president. The people are blocking the highway at every crossroad. They are eager to catch a glimpse of the great man who led our soldiers to victory against the English. Many know and love him. These men crowd to shake his hand and to wish him God speed and blessing in his new task."

Those Who Dared

"My flowers will be all withered then," said Angelica, "and my new dress will be mussed!"

"The flowers will keep, Angelica," her mother replied. "You must learn patience, child. Father has promised to let us know when it is time for you to join the girls." But Angelica was restless. She ran to the window. The streets were crowded. She wanted to join the throng.

After a while, a knock was heard. Angelica flew to the door. There stood her father with ten little girls dressed in white, carrying flowers in their hands.

" 'Tis time to go, Angelica," they cried. "Where are your flowers?"

"Here they are, Angelica," Mrs. Peale said as she handed her excited daughter an armful of beautiful flowers. "And here is the wreath of laurel. I hope it fits the General's head."

Angelica never forgot that day. General Washington rode into Philadelphia on a beautiful horse. With him was the governor of Pennsylvania and soldiers dressed in their best uniforms. The children scattered flowers before the advancing General and his escort, who rode under gaily decorated arches where flags and flowers swayed in the breeze. The crowds sang songs of praise and gratitude for all that Washington had done for the country.

Angelica pressed forward. She did not fear the horses as they carried the escort. We are not told just how it was done. Perhaps someone lifted the little girl up on his shoulder, and General Washington recognized the small daughter of his friend, Mr. Peale, the artist. He

GEORGE WASHINGTON RIDING THROUGH THE STREETS OF PHILADELPHIA ON HIS WAY TO NEW YORK TO BE INAUGURATED AS FIRST PRESIDENT OF THE UNITED STATES

bent forward. Angelica placed her wreath on the great man's head while the people cheered and cheered.

Angelica did not go on with General Washington. So she did not see other girls in Trenton, dressed all in white, strew flowers along his pathway as her friends had done. She did not see the huge barge manned by thirteen pilots dressed in white uniforms, which carried General Washington across the Hudson River to New York. Neither

Those Who Dared

did she hear the cries of welcome, and the boom of the cannon fired in his honor.

She did not see the crowd who cheered as he, preferring to walk, passed through the streets wearing the familiar blue and buff uniform and his three-cornered hat. General Washington was pleased with the joyous reception given him all along the way, but he was sad, too. He wondered if he could guide the newly formed ship of state into peaceful waters. We may see how the great man felt by reading his diary. Here he wrote:

"The boats which attended and joined us on this occasion, the roar of the cannon, the cries of the people, which rent the skies as I passed along the wharves, filled my mind with sensations as painful as they were pleasing."

But Angelica had no such worry. The little girl was tired but happy in her thoughts of how she and her little friends had honored the great General Washington, and how she, of all of them, had placed a crown of laurel upon his head.

CHAPTER XXV

BEGINNINGS OF A NEW NATION

New York City was very gay and colorful on April 30, 1789, when Washington became the first president of the United States. Flags were flying. Flowers and wreaths hung from the windows. Crowds gathered in the streets to see their much loved hero pass to Federal Hall, where he took the oath of office. A gallant figure he was, dressed in dark brown, "with medal [metal] buttons, an eagle on them, white stockings, a bag [wig] and sword." As the oath was taken, the shout arose, "Long live George Washington, President of the United States!"

A few nights later a great ball was given in honor of Washington. Famous men and lovely ladies were there. Each lady received a fan made in Paris with the President's picture painted on ivory.

Soon Mrs. Washington came to the city, and then there were teas, parties, and balls. The people wanted their capital to be as gay and grand as London or Paris.

Washington rode forth in a coach, the finest that had ever been seen in America. This was drawn by four horses except when he went to Federal Hall; then six horses added to the dignity of the President's coming.

Driving on the streets of New York then was not what it is today. Broadway was paved only part of the dis-

IN NEW YORK ON APRIL 30, 1789, GEORGE WASHINGTON TOOK THE OATH OF OFFICE AS PRESIDENT OF THE UNITED STATES

Beginnings of a Nation

tance. Then one had to go through mud. Neither was it pleasant to walk on the streets, particularly at night. The street lamps were far apart and often unlighted. There was danger of slipping into the mud on the poorly paved sidewalk, stumbling against a town pump, or falling over a stray pig in the city streets. The people of New York might receive President Washington royally, but New York was not a great city in the days of the first president.

Members of Congress from the South objected to the long distance from the capital. It took congressmen from the South a month of traveling to attend a session of Congress. So the next year the capital was moved to Philadelphia, while the city of Washington, the future capital of the United States, was being laid out and made ready for the new government.

In the social life at Philadelphia, people still thought of Europe. Dolly Madison wrote, "I went yesterday to see a doll, which has come from England, dressed to show us the fashions."

In the dinners and parties, some delighted to follow the customs from Europe. Mrs. Bingham, who gave beautiful parties, started the custom in this country of having servants announce, or call out, the name of each guest as he arrived.

An amusing story has come to us about this custom. James Monroe had not heard of it. When he entered Mrs. Bingham's door, the servant called out, "Senator Monroe."

Those Who Dared

"Coming," replied Mr. Monroe.

Then another servant down the hall, to let those near him know who was arriving, said, "Senator Monroe."

To this Mr. Monroe hastily answered, "Coming as soon as I can get off my overcoat."

President and Mrs. Washington entered heartily into the ceremony and entertainments of the capital.

Alexander Hamilton, who had charge of the finances of the new nation, also enjoyed the parties, dinners, and balls, and so did his charming wife Elizabeth Schuyler, who was kin to Catalina Schuyler.

But Thomas Jefferson, another of Washington's advisers, who, you remember, wrote the Declaration of Independence, liked a simpler life.

In the beginning of the new nation, these two men, Hamilton and Jefferson, played a most important part. Hamilton thought more of the few wealthy people. He wanted a strong central government made by them. Jefferson thought more of the masses of poor people. He wanted these people to have more rights and a large part in making the government.

Hamilton did a great deal for the country in helping to raise money and form banks during those first years of our government. But Thomas Jefferson, called "The Friend of the People," will live forever in our nation. These two men, in thinking so differently, helped to give a balance to our government.

CHAPTER XXVI

A RIDE IN THE DAYS OF THE FIRST PRESIDENT

Thomas Twining liked to travel. He left England when but a boy and went to live in India. There he became a soldier and fought to gain that country for England.

When he returned to England, he heard all about the Revolutionary War in America. "I want to see the country that dared to fight us," he said. So he set off for America. He kept a diary of his travels, and in this diary, we read:

"April 14, 1796—At ten this morning the negro girl took my bag under her arm and accompanied me to the mail-wagon office. The vehicle was a long car with four benches." Then the diary continues the story of Thomas Twining's journey.

There were no backs to the seats or benches, and this made it very hard to keep one's seat, especially as there was no place for the traveler's bag except under his feet. The light roof of the wagon was upheld by eight posts, four on each side. There were three leather curtains, which came down from the roof, one at each side and one in the back. These curtains rolled up or down to suit the passengers.

When one entered the mail-wagon, he climbed in at

THE "STAGE-WAGON" IN WHICH THOMAS TWINING TRAVELED FROM PHILADELPHIA TO WASHINGTON AND BACK AGAIN IN 1795

the front, stepped over the driver's seat and took whichever place was not occupied. If one came late, he had to take the back seat and thereby had to climb over all the others. The passengers had nothing on which to hold as they bumped over the rough roads. Neither were there any windows through which they could look when the curtains were rolled down.

The driver was not dressed like the English coachman, with great-coat and boots and high hat tilted to one side. Instead he wore a coarse blue jacket, worsted stockings, and thick shoes.

When they came to a river, they drove across on a floating bridge. This was built of large logs laid side by

A Ride in the Early Days

side on the water. Then planks were nailed to the logs. At either bank the bridge was fastened to posts which were sunk deep down into the soft mud. The bridge floated until the wagon touched it, then it sank into the water and mud, splashing it up on the horses and often into the wagon and even on the passengers! No wonder our traveler thought the roads of America were not so good as those of England. However, he very kindly excused our country because it was so young. He wrote he was sure this bridge would soon be replaced by a bridge of stone or brick. There were also some fine wooden and stone bridges in the United States at this time, and Mr. Twining crossed them in his travels.

A short distance from the bridge, the mail-wagon slowed down. The passengers peeped out to see what the trouble was. The driver explained that they had come to a turnpike gate. This meant that the driver had to pay money, or toll, for driving over the bridge. This money was used to buy new logs and planks when the old ones rotted out from being in the water and mud.

They were now coming to the hills. The way was very rough. In the road were huge rocks; on one side were deep cliffs, and on the other, steep hillsides. To avoid the rocks the driver pulled out of the road. Just when Mr. Twining thought they were going over the cliffs the driver pulled them into the hillside and to safety.

It took a mail-wagon two days and half a night to drive from Philadelphia to Baltimore. Today we can go by train in two hours.

Those Who Dared

Mr. Twining made the journey from Philadelphia to Washington because he wanted to see the new capital of the United States. How disappointed he was! He found only a few broad streets laid out "either in the marshy swamp or through what was a forest." There were no buildings as yet in the city, except the beginning of the capitol.

While Mr. Twining was in Washington he was the guest of Mrs. Washington's granddaughter, Mrs. Law. When he returned to Philadelphia, she sent by him a miniature of President Washington to her grandmother.

Mr. Twining enjoyed meeting the great American, George Washington, and his wife. He spoke of Mrs. Washington as a lady whose manner was "kind and unaffected." He wrote of Washington, "So completely did he look the great and good man he really was, that I felt rather respect than awe in his presence. His person was tall and upright. His hair powdered and tied behind. Though his manners were those of a general, the expression of his face had rather a calm dignity of a lawyer than the severity of a soldier."

Judging from what Mr. Twining wrote about his visit to our country, we may believe that perhaps he felt repaid for his rough rides.

CHAPTER XXVII

TWO VIRGINIANS OPEN THE DOOR TO THE WEST

"Captain Clark," called a young soldier on the Ohio River, "the boats are coming! I counted three of them."

Captain William Clark hurried down to the bank of the river. In the distance he recognized his friend, Captain Meriwether Lewis and waved to him. He saw two other flat-bottomed boats following Captain Lewis's boat. These he knew to be loaded with supplies, tools, blankets, and clothing, besides beads, mirrors, and other trinkets for the Indians.

These two Virginians were going on a long trip. Both men were brave soldiers and had fought for their country. Both were hunters, and Captain Lewis had also been secretary to President Jefferson.

Indeed this trip was being taken because President Jefferson wanted to know more about the land west of the Mississippi River which the United States had bought from France. So he had sent for his secretary and said to him, "Captain Lewis, I should like to have you go west into this new country and bring me a report of all you find; describe the land, the mountains, and the rivers and give names to them; keep peace with the Indians; learn their customs and habits. Will you go?"

Captain Lewis had been wishing for a long time to go

Those Who Dared

on such an exploring trip, and so, of course, he agreed to go. Congress gave him the money with which to buy his supplies. He asked his friend, Captain Clark, to go with him and have the same control over the men that he himself had.

Captain Clark wanted to see the Louisiana Purchase, too, as the newly bought land was called. Several other friends from Kentucky were also asked to go with the exploring party.

The two leaders went into camp for the winter in Illinois near the mouth of the Missouri River. Here they enlisted men and trained them for the trip until, one May morning, the welcome order came, "Forward!" The band of more than forty men started their journey up the Missouri River. They saw and talked with Daniel Boone, then seventy years old. The old pioneer was much interested in the journey, which would have delighted him in his younger days.

For days they traveled, seeing only French trappers and a few hunters. These told them that they would find the western Indians different from those in the east. "Be careful of the Sioux," they warned the explorers. "They are the most cruel of all."

The journey up-stream became harder each day. We read in Captain Lewis's diary, "We make only ten miles a day. The men have to push the boats with poles."

You see they were going against the water. There were often great trees floating past them which were dangerous to their light canoes.

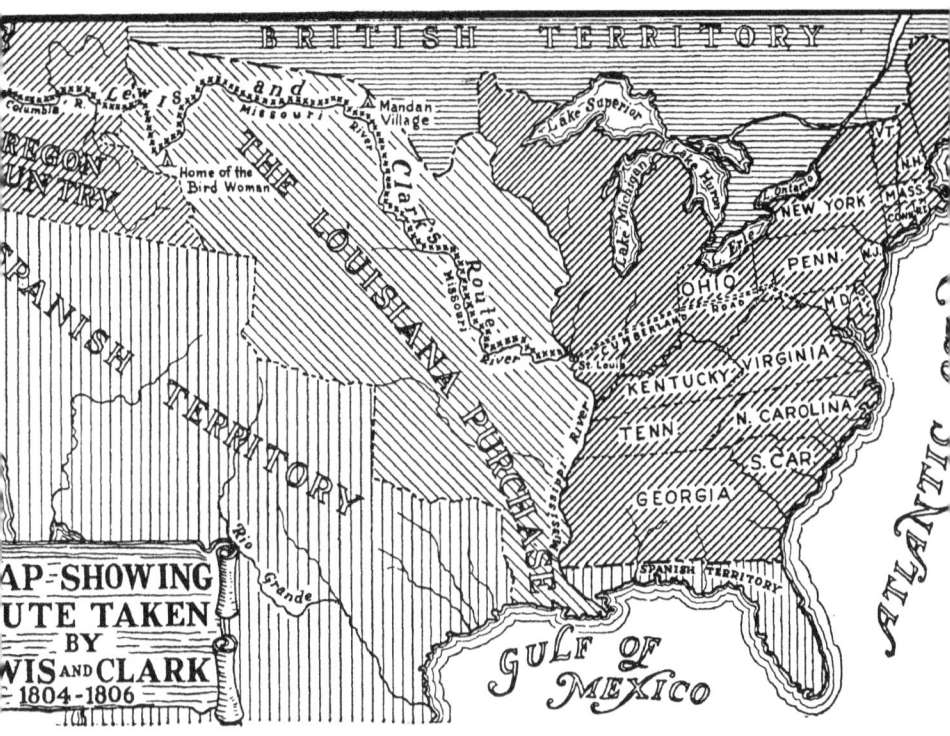

There were sand-bars, too, on which they were often stranded, so that they had to be pushed off. The men worked hard, but they were cheerful. When night came they pitched camp, made a roaring hot fire, and cooked fresh game. One of the men had his old fiddle. While he played, the men danced and sang to his merry tunes.

When Captain Lewis reached the country of the Omaha Indians, he arranged a grand council with them. At this council he told the chiefs that they were no longer children of the French king. They were brothers of the Americans and must look to their Great White Father in Washington for protection. Then the chiefs nodded their heads, smoked their peace pipes, and accepted the presents of the white men. They did not care who owned the land, if they could hunt and fish.

Those Who Dared

The Indians dressed up in the uniforms with red and gilt trimming which Captain Lewis brought. They liked the medals which he gave to them. These had on one side two hands clasped together. This meant peace.

The Indians gave presents, too—soft buffalo blankets and painted skins.

These Indians lived in tents called tepees. These were made of skins which could be hastily put up or pulled down. The Indians had wild little prairie horses and ponies. When the buffalo herds moved about over the prairies, the Indian women and boys quickly pulled down their tents, packed them on the poles, hitched these to their ponies and were off to follow the buffalo. They depended on the buffalo for everything—food, clothing, and weapons.

The explorers next came to the territory of the Sioux Indians. These Indians were not friendly, but Captain Lewis sent for the chief and made him a gift of a "red laced suit, a cocked hat with a red feather in it and an American flag and a white shirt." There were a feast and games and a contest of arrow shooting. In every way the party tried to make friends with the Indians.

AN INDIAN GIRL LENDS A HELPING HAND

One day a Mandan Indian village, far up the Missouri River, was thrown into great excitement. White soldiers in boats had come to their landing. Of course, as you may guess, they were our party of explorers under Captain Lewis and Captain Clark. They had traveled sixteen

The Door to the West

hundred miles up the Missouri River and it was winter once more. They decided to camp here.

The Mandan Indians were friendly. They were very good farmers. They had grain. They welcomed the white men and showed them the pottery which they made from clay. These Indians had warm huts, too, made of poles and brush, and plastered over with clay. These huts had a round roof, with a hole cut in the top to let out the smoke.

The Indians often came to the camp out of curiosity. They liked the white men who were kind and gave them gifts of beads and knives. One day a pretty young squaw visited the camp. Her name was Sa-ca-ja-we-a, which means, "Bird Woman." She saw one of the men grinding corn into meal. She looked at the little mill in amazement.

"Let Sa-ca-ja-we-a try," she begged in broken English. The soldier put a handful of grain into the mill. The squaw turned the handle, and out came the fine meal. This was an easy way to get meal, she thought, for she had to grind and mash her grain between stones.

The soldier gave the mill to Sacajawea. She jumped up and down to show her delight. After this she often came to camp and brought her husband, Charbonneau, with her. Sacajawea told the white men she was not a Mandan Indian. She belonged to the Snake tribe, which lived far, far to the west. She had been captured by enemies who sold her to Charbonneau, a French trapper, and he had married her.

Those Who Dared

This gave Captain Lewis an idea. They would need a guide when they left Fort Mandan. Why not ask Sacajawea to show them the way to her people?

Sacajawea was delighted with the plan. In April she and her husband went with the party. She was the only woman among them, and she carried her tiny papoose strapped to her back.

The explorers were still traveling up-stream. The whirling water made the going very hard. One of the boats turned over. The supplies and the diary of Captain Lewis were swept into the water. Sacajawea saw the papers. She knew they were valuable. She dived into the water and saved those priceless reports. More than once she showed how plucky a woman could be.

One day Captain Lewis heard a queer rumbling noise as he stood alone on the bank. He determined to find out what made that noise. After walking some miles he saw a great waterfall, a sight of wonderful beauty. Before him rose a mist like smoke high into the air. The tints in the spray were like those in the rainbow. The water tumbling over the great rocks into rapids far below made the sound like thunder which he had heard.

While he stood there he saw a herd of buffalo and shot one. As he reloaded his gun, a huge grizzly appeared only a few feet away. Lewis realized his danger. He knew he could not kill it; so he jumped into the river and swam down-stream for some distance before he went ashore.

The men could not take their boats over the falls. They

SACAJAWEA, THE "BIRD WOMAN," GUIDING THE LEWIS AND CLARK EXPEDITION

had to stop and make wagons in which to carry supplies. It was a long eighteen miles around those falls, and the feet of the explorers were torn and sore when they reached the river once more. The men were discouraged too.

Sacajawea comforted them. She told them they would soon find a place where the river "went three ways." That was near her home. When they did come to this spot, Sacajawea jumped up and down in joy. The men called this the Gates to the Rocky Mountains. They named the river, Jefferson, in honor of the President.

Those Who Dared

The party now had to climb up and up. Food was getting scarce. It was only August, but it was already very cold.

"How shall we know when we come to the top of these mountains?" asked one of the soldiers.

"We shall find a stream flowing to the west," Captain Lewis told him. After a few days, the men did find this little stream of sparkling clear water flowing to the west.

Sacajawea, still with her little papoose strapped to her back, now started down the mountain. She knew this country. They saw an Indian coming toward them on horseback. Captain Lewis quickly waved his blanket to show that they were friends. They could see that the Indian was a chief and that there were Indian braves following him.

Sacajawea did a strange thing. She started sucking her fingers. This meant that the Indians belonged to her tribe. Then she danced up and down, for the chief was her own brother.

Sacajawea told the chief all about her white friends. She told him they needed food. Her brother and his men gave the explorers all they needed. He also told the white men about the country. He said they would not be able to take their canoes with them. The river, he said, was full of rocks. The banks were steep rocky walls.

"How do your people get on the other side, then?" Captain Lewis asked Sacajawea.

"They go on foot," she answered. "Carry packs on horses."

The Door to the West

"Then we will go that way too," he said. "Ask your brother to sell us horses."

Through Sacajawea, the men traded beads, mirrors, knives, and blankets for horses, and off they started once more.

THE END OF THE JOURNEY

But Sacajawea did not know the way now. They had to get another guide. The traveling was hard. There was almost no game along their trail. One day there was no food at all.

"What shall we do?" asked the men.

"Kill one of the youngest horses," replied Captain Lewis. "Dress it and cook it. We will soon come to a settlement."

But when they came to the Flat Nose Indian village there was a welcome, but little food. They were living on dried berries, roots, and tea made of bark. Poor food for weary men!

Sacajawea took the berries and made a big pot of hot broth for the men. Then they built canoes and started off once more, down the Snake River. When they came into the Columbia River, they found all the salmon they could eat.

The men were making good time now. They were going down-stream with the current.

At last they saw fog, mist, and gulls. How glad they were! The men were merry. Fog, mist, and gulls meant they were nearing the Pacific Ocean and the end of their journey.

Those Who Dared

The men hoped they would find a ship here at the mouth of the Columbia River which would take them home. Days passed and no ships came. The men built a fort and made camp for the winter. They knew that they could not get back through the mountains then.

One day a whale was washed up on the beach. The soldiers went running, for food was low. Sacajawea strapped her papoose on her back and ran too.

"No go, Sacajawea," said one of the men. "You stay here—keep fort." Sacajawea was hurt. She burst into tears and ran to Captain Lewis. She said she had traveled a long way to see the Great Water and now that a great fish was to be seen too, she thought it very hard not to be allowed to see either. So she was allowed to go along.

It was a bitter cold winter. Once the men were so hungry that they went to an Indian village where they ate roasted dogs.

The Return Home

When April came, the men broke camp and started back home. Sacajawea, the brave guide, with her husband and little papoose returned with the party to her home at the Mandan village. She had seen the "Great Water" and had visited her brother, but she did not care to stay with her native Indian tribe. When her little son was older, they lived in St. Louis, where he attended school, but after this they again went back to their home among the Indians.

The exploring party returned to St. Louis after an absence of two and a half years. Many of their friends

The Door to the West

had given them up for lost. What a hearty welcome our heroes now received!

But Captain Lewis and Captain Clark hastened on to Washington, where they made their reports to the President. He was more than pleased with what the men had found out about the great West.

CHAPTER XXVIII

THE LAST OF THE PIRATES TURN PATRIOTS

"Pirates! Pirates!" was a cry all vessels feared as they neared the Gulf of Mexico. And well they might, for in 1809 the pirates were as bold and cruel as were Blackbeard and Captain Kidd almost a hundred years before.

These pirates were two French brothers, Jean and Pierre Lafitte, who had come to America. At first they were content to smuggle in slaves, which they sold to the plantation owners. Then the pirates grew bolder and lay in wait for merchant vessels from every country. These they robbed and carried off the cargoes to their den.

This den was on a little bay which was just off the Gulf of Mexico not far from New Orleans. It was well hidden by the tall trees of Grand Island. There the high masts of the boats could not be seen while the pirates unloaded and put the cargoes in the long low warehouse.

Jean Lafitte was in charge at Grand Island. He directed the pirates and sent the stolen goods down a number of little streams, like a back-stairs, to New Orleans. When the men reached New Orleans, they took the goods to a blacksmith shop.

The other brother, Pierre Lafitte, stayed in the blacksmith shop. He managed the slaves who forged the iron there. He traded with the sea captains, sailors, and mer-

JEAN LAFITTE ANSWERS GOVERNOR CLAIBORNE

Those Who Dared

chants who came to bargain and haggle over the prices of the stolen goods.

The pirates grew wealthy. They grew bolder. They held auction sales and openly advertised these sales all over New Orleans.

The merchants could not sell what they had in their shops. Their customers were buying from the pirates at lower prices.

The custom house in New Orleans also began to lose money because they did not get the tax which they should be getting from goods brought into the country. The United States government missed this money. So the order came to capture the pirates.

A pirate boat was sighted. A fight followed. The government men were defeated, and one man was badly wounded.

This was too much for Governor Claiborne. He offered a reward for the capture of Jean Lafitte. Jean read the notice and laughed. Soon another notice appeared by this one. It was a reward offered for capturing the governor and signed by Jean Lafitte. People read this and laughed at the boldness of the man.

Governor Claiborne waited. Then he arrested Pierre Lafitte in his blacksmith shop and put him in jail.

Jean came to the defense of his brother. He employed two of the best lawyers in New Orleans. One was District Attorney John Grimes.

"I will pay you $20,000," said Jean Lafitte, "to defend my brother."

Pirates Turn Patriots

And John Grimes resigned his job to defend the pirate.

"You bartered away your honor," reproached the lawyer on the opposite side, "for pirates' gold."

But Pierre Lafitte escaped from prison before the trial.

About this time, England and America were at war. The English had been seizing American merchant vessels and searching them, and had often made the American sailors work on English ships. The English had a base for supplies in Florida, which was then owned by Spain.

The English were planning to attack New Orleans. They wanted to get Jean Lafitte to guide them down his back-stairs to the city, so that they could capture it before the Americans could defend themselves.

One day an English vessel sailed up to Grand Island and fired a cannon. Jean went down and met the officers and took them to his house, where he gave them a fine dinner. Then an officer gave Jean a letter from the commander in Florida. He offered Jean $30,000 and a captaincy in the English navy if Jean would help the English attack New Orleans.

Jean asked the officer to excuse him while he talked the matter over with his friends. While he was out, his men seized the Englishmen and put them in jail and tied up their vessel where it could not be seen from the Gulf.

When Jean returned, he went to the jail and let the Englishmen out. He apologized for his men. He asked the officer to give his compliments to his commander and tell him that he would let him have a reply in a short time.

THE PIRATES TURN PATRIOTS AND DEFEND NEW ORLEANS FROM THE BRITISH IN THE WAR OF 1812

Jean Lafitte then wrote to Governor Claiborne and sent him the letter he had received from the English. He offered to fight for the United States and help protect New Orleans if he and his men could be pardoned. Governor Claiborne did not reply.

Soon General Jackson came with a small force to defend the city. He lost no time in making plans to save New Orleans from the English, but there were few men and not enough arms and powder.

Lafitte saw that he had one more chance. He decided to go to General Jackson and offer his men and their supply of arms. This he did, and Jackson accepted his offer with thanks.

Pirates Turn Patriots

These pirates knew how to fight. Very bravely now did they come to the defense of their country and city. On the morning of the battle Jackson said, "I wish I had fifty guns with five hundred such fellows behind them."

The guns of the pirate patriots flashed and thundered. They mowed down the marching columns of the red-coated English soldiers. The English columns crumpled like paper dolls. In less than ten minutes the pride of the English navy was compelled to retreat.

But they soon returned bringing their hard-won cannon from their ships in the harbor. The pirates were unafraid. They calmly shot at the guns and blew them up. Again and again the English commander tried to rally his men. Then he was killed, and the English retreated.

At last on January 17, the English vessels sailed out from the harbor and home to England.

President Madison granted the pirates a full pardon, "with generous forgiveness."

And so the last of the pirates became patriots.

We wish that the story ended here. For Jean Lafitte was as charming and generous as he was bold and fearless. Many of the pirates whom President Madison pardoned remained loyal citizens. But Pierre and Jean Lafitte left New Orleans and again became pirates.

THE LIBRARY

Stories in Other Books

"George Washington, Our First President," "How a Capital City Was Chosen, in *Makers of the Nation*, by Fanny E. Coe.

Those Who Dared

"George Washington, Our First President," in *The Story of Virginia*, by Carrie Hunter Willis and Lucy S. Saunders.

"George Washington, Father of His Country," in *Makers of Our History*, by John Thomson Faris.

"New Ways of Travel Needed," "Roads," "The Experience of Charles Dickens," "Thomas Jefferson," in *Makers of Our Nation*, by Reuben Post Halleck and Juliette Frantz.

"Thomas Jefferson and the Louisiana Purchase," in *American Leaders and Heroes*, by Wilbur Fisk Gordy.

"Stories about Jefferson," "A Long Journey," "Captain Clark's Burning Glass," in *Stories of Great Americans for Little Americans*, by Edward Eggleston.

"The Landlord's Mistake," "The Surly Guest," in *Fifty Famous People*, by James Baldwin.

"Meriwether Lewis and William Clark," in *Virginia And Her Builders*, by Mabel Flick Altstetter and Richard Lee Morton.

"The Lewis and Clark Expedition," in *Our Nation Grows Up*, by Eugene C. Barker.

"Lewis and Clark—Explorers," in *Stories of Early Times in the Great West for Young Readers*, by Florence Bass.

"Governor Spotswood and Blackbeard the Pirate," in *The Story of Virginia*.

"Blackbeard the Last of the Pirates," in *Founders of Our Country*, by Fanny E. Coe.

"Blackbeard, The Pirate," in *The Days of Yester-Year, a Sketch Book of Virginia*, by W. H. T. Squires.

Self-Testing Game

This is another word game. From the following list find the word that makes the sentence true. Each correct sentence counts 2. (The words are: Federal Hall, pirates, lamp-post, pig, war, Sacajawea, New York, two, thirteen sailors, floating, Louisiana territory.)

1. Great crowds greeted Washington on his way to —— —— to become our first president.

A New Nation

2. A barge manned by —— —— dressed in white took him across the harbor.

3. After Washington took the oath of office at —— ——, he was greeted by cheers from the people.

4. In those days the streets of New York were dimly lighted. At night one might stumble against a —— —— or a stray ——.

5. At that time there were in the country some —— bridges.

6. When Jefferson was president the United States bought the —— ——.

7. On their trip to the Pacific Coast, Lewis and Clark were gone more than —— years.

8. ——, a young Indian woman, helped to guide the way.

9. Long ago —— hid on the coast and robbed ships.

10. The United States had another —— with England in 1812.

The highest possible score is 20. What is your score?

Choose Something to Do

1. Make a Hall of Fame in one corner of your room. In this corner place the pictures of those who helped in building the new nation. Under each picture write a statement telling why this person should be in the Hall of Fame.

2. Divide your class into three groups. Let each dramatize scenes: One from "A Little Girl Crowns a President"; another from "An Indian Girl Lends a Helping Hand"; others from "The Last of the Pirates Turn Patriots."

3. Pirate stories are listed in "Stories in Other Books." Some members of your class might read these or other pirate stories and tell them to the class.

4. Make riddles about people in this Part, "Our Country— A New Nation." See if your classmates can guess the riddles.

PART VII

PIONEERS! MORE PIONEERS!

CHAPTER XXIX

PEOPLE GO WEST

Rafts, flat-boats, covered wagons, ox-carts, riders, walkers! So thousands of people found their way to the West. Lewis and Clark returned from the Pacific Coast and told of the great country west of the Mississippi. The war of 1812 was over. During the hard times that followed, people decided to try their fortune in a new country where land was rich and cheap and game abundant.

At first they settled Ohio, Kentucky, Tennessee and the country east of the Mississippi. Later they crossed the river to the west and southwest. Many cabins were left deserted and were marked "Gone to Texas."

Even to the people of that day, the pictures made by others in their rush to the West seemed amusing. One man wrote, "Today we passed two large rafts lashed together." On these several families from New England were carrying their property down the Ohio "to the land of promise in the western woods." Each raft was eighty or ninety feet long, with a small house built on it, "and on each was a stack of hay, round which several horses and cows were feeding." The ploughs, wagons, pigs, chickens, and children looked more like a home farm-yard scene than a group of adventurers seeking a new home. On one raft, an old lady with spectacles was

DOWN THE OHIO IN HUGE FLATBOATS FLOATED THE PIONEERS BY TENS OF THOUSANDS, WITH THEIR POTS AND PANS AND LIVESTOCK

seated on a chair at the door of the cabin, quietly knitting; another woman was at the wash-tub; the men were standing around talking and chewing tobacco, and the work of the family "seemed to go on like clock-work."

Hundreds of other settlers were making their way down the Ohio River on flat-bottomed boats. In these were loaded the horses, the cattle, and whatever the people felt would be needed in their new homes in the West. These flat-boats drifted with the flow of the stream. They were guided chiefly by a long sweep at

People Go West

the end of the boat. These sweeps were very hard to handle. No wonder the people sang,

"The boatmen dance, the boatmen sing,
The boatmen can do most anything."

The families who floated down the river had an easier time than those who followed the Wilderness Road or made their way through unbroken forest. These traveled on horseback and in covered wagons. Into the wagons were crowded perhaps a piece of treasured furniture, bed covers, clothes, with boxes in which there were perhaps a few books. Some carried window glass for their home in the wilderness. The pot and the frying pan went with every group of pioneers. Sometimes, to give more room, these were hung on the outside of the wagon. Cattle followed the wagon. Where numbers of settlers joined together for protection to follow the western trails, it looked indeed as if "America was moving west."

Some were not so fortunate as to travel in a covered wagon. A note written at that time says, there passed through a town in Georgia "a man and his wife, his son and wife with a cart but no horse. The man had a belt over his shoulders and he drew in the shafts; the son worked by traces to the end of the shafts and helped his father to draw the cart; the son's wife rode in the cart, and the old woman was walking carrying a rifle and driving a cow."

When pioneers reached the spot in the forest where they decided to make their new homes, trees were cut and cabins built. A log cut in half made the table. Three-

MANY PIONEERS FOLLOWED THE OVERLAND TRAIL IN COVERED WAGONS

legged stools were their chairs. Often the beds were only bunks built on the side of the wall. Over every fireplace or by the door hung the gun.

When the settlers went into the prairie states, there were no trees with which to build log cabins. They made houses of grass sod, and so "soddies" instead of "log cabins" sprang up on the plains of the west. To protect themselves from the hard storms that sometimes swept over these treeless plains, they had "dugouts" in the ground into which they could run for safety.

Each group of settlers had its own story, but there were many more hardships than pleasures in the rough life of pioneer days.

CHAPTER XXX

A FAMOUS GUIDE AND A PATHFINDER

Kit Carson was tired of cutting the tough leather with which he made harness and mended worn saddles. He was tired of the musty smell of leather in Mr. Workman's harness shop in Franklin, Missouri. He was tired of being an "apprentice boy," as he was called while he learned a trade.

Yet Christopher, which was his real name, was not quite sixteen years old. He felt that he was a man, because he had been working for almost two years at his trade.

Many men came to Mr. Workman's shop. Some of these were from the East, and they stopped to ask about the Santa Fé Trail, which began at Franklin. But these men from the East did not interest Kit so much as did those from the West, dressed in checkered, hand-woven woolen shirts and tight-fitting leather pants, and wearing rawhide boots. These men were trappers who traveled back and forth between Franklin and the far West. They told Kit thrilling stories of buffalo stampedes, of adventures in trapping, of capturing wild ponies on the plains, and of the strange Indians and Mexicans whom they met in Santa Fé, which then belonged to Mexico, the Spanish country to the southwest.

Kit became more restless. He felt that life in a saddle shop was too tame for a man. His time was not up in

KIT CARSON LEAVES HOME TO JOIN A TRADERS' CARAVAN ON THE SANTA FÉ TRAIL

Mr. Workman's shop, and he knew that neither his father nor his master would let him go. So Kit ran away.

Mr. Workman advertised in the newspaper, the *Missouri Intelligencer* for his run-away apprentice and offered one cent reward for his return. But no one bothered to catch Kit, who joined a party of trappers bound for the settlement at Santa Fé.

Kit knew that there were dangers all along the way, for there were no charts or maps of the trails. The men would have to find their own water and pastures for their pack horses.

A Guide and a Pathfinder

The captain of the trappers was as strict as an officer in the army. The twenty men had to obey his orders. Each man was armed and could shoot his mark. Each led his own pack-horse or mule which was laden with provisions and with goods such as needles, mirrors, and other things to tempt the Indians and Mexicans to trade for furs.

Every morning Kit and the men were awakened at dawn by a boy blowing a bugle. Then the men hastily dressed and ate breakfast and began their long march. At noon they rested for two hours while some of them prepared and cooked the game which they had shot along the march.

The men pushed on with their faces always toward the sinking sun. Before it set, they found a good camping place. The mules were tied to stakes or trees, and once more there was a camp fire and a guard posted to watch for Indians or other enemies. The men sang and told stories until it was bedtime. Kit's journey was not so full of danger as he had thought it would be, and he reached Santa Fé safely.

Kit was in a different world now. He heard a strange language which he was told was Spanish. Some Mexicans spoke the Indian language too. He listened closely to them and watched their faces to learn whether they were friendly or not. Kit saw strange houses made of clay which had been baked in the hot sun. He watched the Mexicans and Indians bring in game from their hunts, and soon he was hunting with them.

IN SANTA FÉ KIT CARSON MEETS KIN CADE

Kit Carson Meets Kin Cade

But Kit decided he would go farther west. He met an older man, named Kin Cade, who was a famous hunter. They liked each other, and Kin asked Kit to spend the winter with him in his mountain hut. Kit agreed and paid for his room and board with his gun.

Kin told Kit that he must learn to speak Spanish and the Indian language if he would trade with the trappers. He taught Kit Spanish and told about the customs of the people. He taught Kit how to trap the fur-bearing animals and how to tan the skins so that they would be soft

A Guide and a Pathfinder

and easy to handle. He showed Kit how to cut and tailor the leather hunting-coats and tight-fitting breeches.

Kit slept upon a bed made of posts. In this bed corn shucks were packed and then covered with a buffalo robe. The men burned huge pine knots during the winter to light their cabin. Kit for the first time was having real lessons though they did not seem like lessons to him. Kit was learning geography. Kin told him of the country round about them. He would take his hand-carved cane and draw a map on the dirt floor for Kit. Here, he told Kit, were the mountain peaks of the Rocky Mountains. Here were the rivers and valleys and wild canyons. Kit determined to explore this country. So when spring came, he left his friend and started off.

Kit tramped over a thousand miles through the prairies and wilderness. He heard the howling wolves and coyotes. He shot bears, buffaloes, and deer. He met and talked to many different tribes of Indians. After sixteen years of scouting and trapping, Kit returned to Missouri.

What a changed place he found in Franklin! His old home was deserted. Many of his family were dead. He saw few whom he knew. The town had grown larger. It all made Kit sad; so he left and went to St. Louis. There he stayed for two weeks sight-seeing. He heard that a steamboat was leaving, and decided to make a trip on it.

A Guide for a Pathfinder

This was in the early days of the steamboat. On other pages you will read the story of Fulton's first steamboat.

KIT CARSON LEARNS TO BE A HUNTER AND TRAPPER

A Guide and a Pathfinder

Kit was very much interested in the wonderful boat on which he found himself. He had to go all over it and see especially the engine. When he came out on the deck once more, he noticed a man talking to a group of men who were listening attentively to all he said. Kit joined the group, and after a while he found that the man was Lieutenant John C. Frémont. He was being sent by the United States government to explore the passes in the great Rocky Mountains. He was going to make maps of the rivers, mountains, and valleys.

Kit heard him say, "I have everything ready for my trip. All I need is an expert guide."

Kit decided to tell Lieutenant Frémont that he would guide him on his trip. Frémont was delighted, and after asking Kit several questions accepted his offer.

Kit was now doing work which he loved. He led the party through the South Pass to the Rocky Mountains. They climbed the highest peak in Wyoming and placed a United States flag upon it and named it for Frémont, who made a map of all that country as they went along.

The next year Frémont and his men spent months in the Sierra Nevada Mountains. There they were caught in a blizzard. The snow piled higher and higher. The men were prisoners in the drifts. They suffered as they dug a path through the great piles of snow. They were half starved, too, for their food had almost given out. But at last they reached California, where they found fish and game.

Frémont was happy. His maps of the country were

KIT CARSON GUIDES JOHN CHARLES FRÉMONT, "THE PATHFINDER," ON SOME OF HIS MOST FAMOUS EXPLORATIONS

finished, and he knew that now the settlers who were eager to go into the far North and West would have a map which would show them where to find water, game, and pasture lands along the way. Kit Carson, the guide, had helped Frémont, the pathfinder, whose maps were used by thousands of pioneers as they pushed farther and farther west.

CHAPTER XXXI

THE FATHER OF TEXAS, STEPHEN F. AUSTIN

"We are moving again, wife," said Mr. Moses Austin one morning to his wife. "I hear there is a fortune to be made in the lead mines in Missouri."

Mrs. Austin did not object. She knew her husband had made up his mind to "pioneer" once more. She had not been in Virginia very long, but she liked her home in Wythe County where her little boy, Stephen, was born.

But Stephen could remember little about the long ride over the mountains through Tennessee or the trip across the river before the family reached Missouri.

Mr. and Mrs. Austin sent Stephen to Connecticut to school when he was only eleven years old. Then when he was fifteen they sent him to an academy in Kentucky, and there he stayed until he was graduated.

We are told that Stephen was a quiet boy and studied hard. He liked the other boys and made friends easily. He read all the books he could find and studied law. When he was only twenty years old, he was making laws in the legislature of Missouri.

His father heard about the rich lands in Texas, and he made up his mind to go there. He went first to New Orleans and from there to Texas. He saw that it was a country of wide rich plains and valleys and rolling rivers.

Those Who Dared

He began to dream of taking hundreds of Americans and forming a colony in Texas. Texas at this time belonged to Mexico, but Moses Austin got permission from the governor of Mexico to take three hundred settlers into Texas.

Before he could carry out his plans, he was taken ill. Just before he died, he begged his wife to tell his son, Stephen, to carry on the work of settling Texas.

Stephen was already in Texas when he received the news of his father's death, and he took up his father's work and spent the rest of his life in carrying it on.

He found that many Americans were eager to go to Texas. They went from Kentucky, Tennessee, Arkansas, and other states. It was easy for the people of Louisiana to step across an imaginary line and find themselves in Texas. In a very short time, Austin had the names of more than enough people to make up his colony of three hundred.

This colony was near the Gulf of Mexico, between the Brazos River and the Colorado River, and the settlers went there by different routes. Some went overland, but many went down the Mississippi and then sailed west along the coast of the Gulf of Mexico until they reached the mouth of the Brazos River or the Colorado River. Then they would land and find their way to the new colony.

Austin made one of his trips from New Orleans to his colony in the steamboat "Beaver." He sent one of the first parties of settlers in a small sailing ship called the

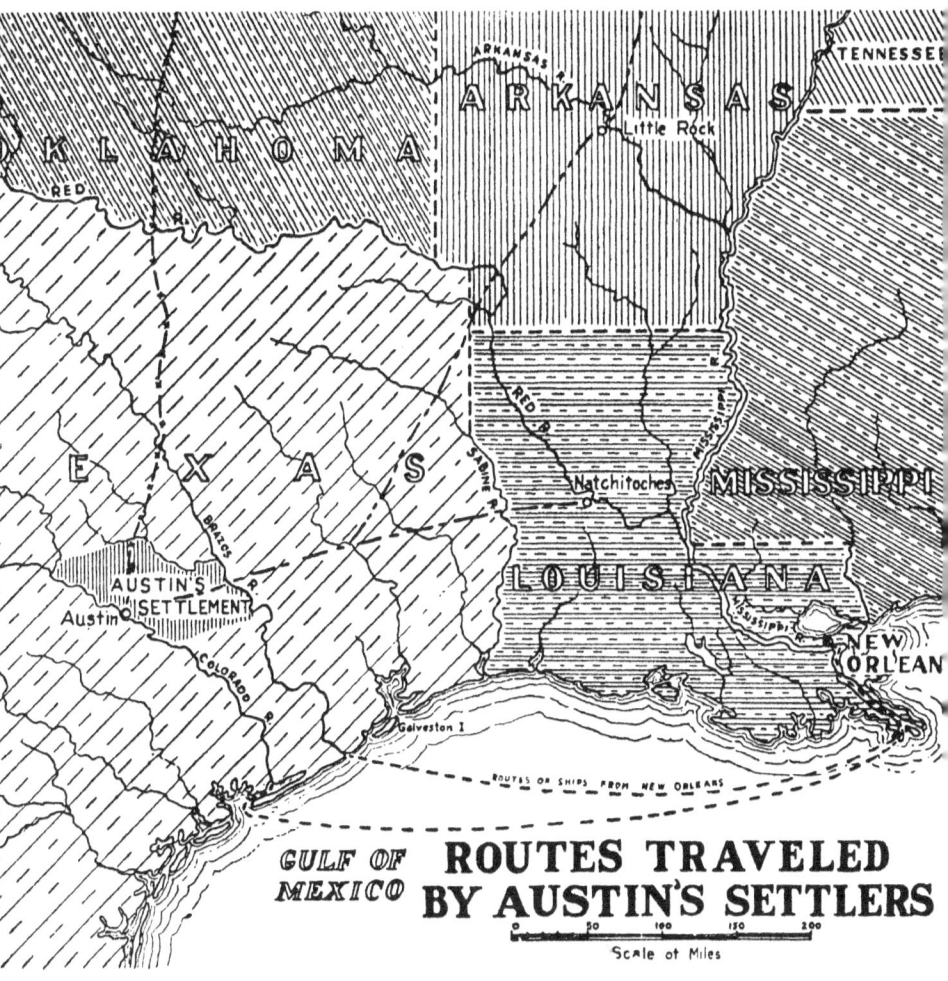

ROUTES TRAVELED BY AUSTIN'S SETTLERS

"Lively." On its second trip, with more settlers, the "Lively" was wrecked on Galveston Island. The cargo was lost, but the passengers were rescued by the schooner "John Motley."

What adventures these Texas pioneers had! One party lost their salt. Their grain gave out and they had no bread. Their only food for a while was the game the men killed along the way.

Each man who settled in Texas promised that he would live according to the laws of Mexico, and most of them

Those Who Dared

kept their pledges to their new country. Many Americans continued to come from the United States. Mexico began to fear these ever-growing crowds. The Mexicans made stricter laws for the Americans. They even demanded that the Americans should give up their guns. These the Americans needed, not only to protect themselves from the Indians and bandit Mexicans, but to provide food for their families.

Stephen Austin went to Mexico City and pleaded with the Mexican government not to be so hard on the Americans. He did all he could to prevent the war which was threatening the future of his colony. He was thrown into prison. Months passed before he was released. Upon his return to Texas, he decided to lead his colony in their fight for independence. He was dearly beloved by all who knew him and the city of Austin, Texas, is named in his honor. He has been called "The Father of Texas" because of his devotion to his people at all times.

CHAPTER XXXII

THE ALTAR OF TEXAS FREEDOM

"What is that Mexican saying?" asked one of the American soldiers within the Texas fort.

"He is speaking Spanish," replied his friend. "He says his General, Santa Anna, demands the surrender of our fort!"

"Listen," said the first. "General Travis is speaking."

"I shall never surrender!" spoke General Travis quietly.

"We shall never surrender!" shouted his loyal men.

It was spring in southern Texas. The flowers were blooming though it was in February. There were over one hundred and fifty American soldiers in the Alamo mission, which they had turned into a fort.

These Americans were all soldiers except Mrs. Dickinson and her tiny baby and a Negro man who belonged to General Travis.

Now General Travis and his small band of American soldiers were surrounded by Santa Anna and his army. For two weeks the Mexicans camped on all sides. They marched around and around the little fort of the Americans.

General Travis wrote several letters which he sent out by brave men at night. Let us read one of his own accounts:

Those Who Dared

"I am besieged under Santa Anna. I have answered the demands to surrender by shooting our cannon and waving our flag proudly from our walls. I shall never surrender nor retreat! Victory or Death!"

Then he wrote describing how the Mexicans marched around and around the fort: "Two hundred shells fell on the Alamo and not one man was hurt, though the Americans' guns killed many of the Mexicans."

A few days later Travis wrote another letter, asking for more soldiers to be sent to help him:

"I am still here and in fine spirits. I have one hundred and forty men and have held this place for ten days against fifteen hundred to six thousand Mexicans. Shall continue to hold it till I get relief from my countrymen or I will perish in its defense."

But alas! This was the last ever heard from the brave General Travis or any of his men.

The Mexicans cut off all the ways by which the Americans could get water. Then they began to storm the Alamo. The Mexicans put up high ladders against the church walls. As fast as they climbed, the Americans shot them down.

"Boys," said General Travis, "we are far outnumbered, but we will make a victory worse to the enemy than defeat!" He stood on the wall and fought side by side with his American soldiers. He cheered them by shouting, "Hurrah, my boys!" until he was shot.

Four hundred of the Mexicans brought more ladders and charged once more the Alamo walls. This time there

"REMEMBER THE ALAMO!"

were not a hundred and forty Americans. Many were wounded. They could not re-load their guns fast enough to shoot down the enemy. Now there were so many Mexicans that the Americans had to beat them off with the butt ends of their guns. Slowly but steadily the Mexicans battered down the wounded Americans until not one could raise his arms to defend himself.

Mrs. Dickinson, her baby, and the Negro man escaped death. They returned worn and dazed to their American friends and told the horrible story of the Alamo.

Those Who Dared

"The Alamo has fallen!" was the cry which swept across the Texas valley and plains.

"Never surrender or retreat!" echoed from cabin to cabin. Men and boys rushed forth to fight for liberty and to avenge the deaths of those brave Americans who had given their lives at the Alamo.

"Remember the Alamo!" was the new battle cry, and under the command of General Sam Houston, the Americans won their independence from Mexico.

THE LIBRARY
Stories in Other Books

"America Moves West," in *These United States and How They Came to Be,* by Gertrude Hartman.

"Frémont, the Pathfinder And His Guide, Kit Carson," "Wonderful News from the Frontier," "Striving Times in the Southwest," in *Makers of the Nation,* by Fanny E. Coe.

"Christopher Carson," in *Makers of Our Nation,* by Reuben Post Halleck and Juliette Frantz.

"A Story of Early Times," "Grandfather's Story," *Stories of Pioneer Life for Young Readers,* by Florence Bass.

Letters of Polly, the Pioneer, by Stella Humphrey Nida.

"The Story of the First White Men in Texas," in *Our Nation Begins,* by Eugene C. Barker, William E. Dodd, and Walter P. Webb.

SELF-TESTING GAME

This is another matching game. On a separate sheet of paper place the beginning of each sentence with the right ending. Each correct sentence counts 2.

Beginnings

1. One reason people went west was
2. They traveled

Pioneers! More Pioneers!

3. Frémont was
4. Kit Carson was
5. Trappers traded trinkets
6. Moses Austin planned
7. Stephen Austin carried on
8. The Mexicans became
9. Strict laws were
10. The Texans

Endings

made against the Texans.
a guide and hunter.
to settle a colony in Texas.
because of cheap land.
a pathfinder for country in the West.
in flatboats and covered wagons.
with the Indians for furs.
his father's plans.
won their freedom.
alarmed at the number of American settlers.

Check your work. The highest possible score is 20.

Choose Something to Do

1. It would be interesting to have "Living Pictures of Pioneer Days." Some of your classmates could represent different people; others could represent pioneer scenes. This would be something like a pantomime. The pupils would act but not speak.
2. Draw pictures of the pioneers:
    a. Moving to homes in the West—in covered wagons, or on flat-boats.
    b. The pioneer home—the furniture, preparing a meal.
    c. Work of pioneer men—clearing the forest, hunting, protecting their homes from the Indians.
3. Carl Sandburg has collected in his *American Song Bag*

Those Who Dared

some pioneer songs. You might enjoy singing some of these: "Old Brass Wagon," "Little Old Sod Shanty," "Turkey in the Straw," "She [The Stagecoach] Is Coming Round the Corner."

4. You might build a flatboat, a covered wagon, and a log cabin. Pioneer people could be made and a pioneer scene constructed.

PART VIII

SOMETHING NEW

CHAPTER XXXIII

MAKING A MILL FROM MEMORY

Did you ever play a memory game? You are told to look closely at a number of objects on a table for five minutes, and then turn your back and write down the names of all you remember.

Once there was a young man who looked and studied parts of a machine and memorized them just as you would in a game. His name was Samuel Slater, and he lived in England.

When Samuel was a young boy his parents bound him out to learn a trade. He was called an apprentice. Samuel liked Mr. Strutt, who owned the mill where he worked. Samuel knew that his master had invented a stocking-frame, on which ribbed stockings could be knit.

One day Samuel met another inventor, Mr. Arkwright, who came to the old English town. He brought a new invention to Mr. Strutt. It was a spinning frame. Mr. Arkwright claimed that it could spin cotton into thread much faster than it had ever been done before, and that the thread would be smoother and stronger. Mr. Arkwright proved to Mr. Strutt that his machine was practical. The two men built a larger mill, and Samuel was delighted when he was given a job in the new mill. It is said that he helped Mr. Strutt and Mr. Arkwright to improve their machines.

Those Who Dared

One day Samuel heard news from far-away America. He read that the State of Pennsylvania had given $500 to a man who had invented the carding machine. Samuel decided that he would go to America. He would build a spinning machine and have mills in the new country, and he would grow to be a rich man.

But many things arose to make his going difficult. First, England watched her inventions carefully. She did not allow anyone to draw pictures of her machines. She did not permit anyone to build models or toy machines to be taken out of the country. No one was allowed even to write and describe a machine.

Samuel Slater knew this. Day by day he looked at the machines when they were still. He watched them when they were working at full speed and were only a shining blur. Then he shut his eyes and tried to picture each part in his memory. At night he went over and over how the pieces fitted together. He dreamed about them.

At last he felt that he had memorized each part and knew how it worked with the other parts. Then he packed a very few clothes and dressed himself like a simple farmer, for a mill worker was not allowed to leave England. His disguise succeeded, and he sailed for America.

Samuel Slater went to Pawtucket, Rhode Island, and there began working on his machine from memory. It was not easy. He had to make each piece himself. Sometimes he had to make one part again and again because it would not fit or work with the other parts.

AN EARLY NEW ENGLAND COTTON MILL

But his determination and patience won. At the end of a year his machine was ready. The mill had been built in the meantime near a stream. The water was turned on, and his wheels began to whir. His machines worked! Business came in faster than he could get his cotton woven. He sent for his brother John to come over from England. Then the Slater brothers built more and more mills and more factories all over New England.

Samuel Slater's wife came over soon after he arrived in Rhode Island. She did all she could to encourage her husband. She had good ideas, too, and her husband knew

Making a Mill from Memory

that they were good. One day she told him how tedious it was to wind a hank of thread to use in sewing. In those days there were no spools of thread for sewing as we have today. Thread was made from linen flax. This was twisted by hand and came in huge hanks, like some wool which you see today. Mrs. Slater asked her husband to try making sewing-thread from cotton. He, with her help, worked out her ideas until he made the cotton into thread which was later put on spools.

The Slater mills needed many bales of cotton and many pounds of wool. So more and more cotton was grown in the South, and more sheep were raised in other parts of the country. Many young women were finding work in the New England factories. So you can see that the English boy, Samuel Slater, had a great effect on life in our country.

When Samuel Slater died, he left a large fortune to his nephew, John Slater, and John Slater made a great deal of money of his own. Now part of this large fortune is called the Slater Fund. It is still being used to teach the Negroes in the South how to do all kinds of useful work with their hands.

CHAPTER XXXIV

ELI WHITNEY INVENTS THE COTTON GIN

One day Mrs. Greene, at her home near Savannah, Georgia, had as her guests several soldiers and planters. These gentlemen were her neighbors from near-by plantations. The conversation turned to their crops, especially that of cotton. Cotton was the "money crop" which was shipped to northern markets.

"If only some way could be found to get the seeds separated from the cotton," said a planter, "we could grow more cotton, now that there is a greater demand for it. That new invention which came from England, a machine which spins and weaves faster than the old hand looms, has created a demand for cotton."

"Oh," cried Mrs. Greene, "why not ask my young friend, Eli Whitney, to help us. He can do anything with his hands. He has made all kinds of toys for my children and he made me the best embroidery frame I have ever seen. I will send for him." Mrs. Greene sent a Negro servant with a request to Mr. Whitney to meet her friends.

While they waited for him, Mrs. Greene told her neighbors something about Mr. Whitney. She had met him a short while before on the boat coming down from Massachusetts to Savannah. Mr. Whitney had come south to teach the children of a man in Savannah.

Those Who Dared

Imagine his surprise when he found the position already filled. Mr. Whitney was left in a strange town without money for his trip back to his home in Westboro, Massachusetts. Knowing that he wished to become a lawyer, Mrs. Greene had invited him to stay with them and read law until he could earn money with which to study.

"Gentlemen," said Mrs. Greene, as Mr. Whitney came into the room, "this is my friend, Mr. Whitney. Explain what you need. I am sure he can make it for you!"

"Will you make a machine for us which will get the seeds from the cotton?" spoke a practical planter. "We have a chance to make more from our cotton crops now that you New Englanders are putting in those new spinning machines. But we have such a time getting the cotton ready! Each boll has to be picked by hand. The fastest seed-picker can separate only a few pounds a day."

Mr. Whitney explained he knew very little about cotton. He promised he would get a ripe boll and study it carefully, which he did. He slowly pulled the boll apart. Then he saw how tightly the fine threads or fibres stuck to the tiny seeds. He realized some kind of fingers would have to be put in his machine.

Mrs. Greene gave him a room in her basement for his workshop. There in a short time he had made his cotton gin. "Gin" is a short form of the word "engine." Mrs. Greene and the children were almost as interested in it as was Mr. Whitney. When the gin was finished, all of the family went in to see how it worked.

The cotton was brought in and placed in the hopper.

ELI WHITNEY'S COTTON GIN IS SUCCESSFUL

The sides were made of iron. Within the hopper was a long round wooden arm called a cylinder. This was filled with hundreds of tiny wire teeth which curved backwards as the cylinder turned. Mr. Whitney began to turn the handle. Soon the children saw the snow white cotton coming through the slits in the iron bars. They laughed and shouted, "It works, mama. The gin works!"

Mrs. Greene was as excited as the children. They bent nearer to watch how the wire teeth in the cylinders tore the cotton from the seeds while the pressure forced the soft fibres between the slits, but the seeds could not get through.

Those Who Dared

But Mr. Whitney soon had trouble. He could not turn the handle as easily as before. When he examined the cylinder, he found that the seed had got in between all the tiny wire teeth. These seeds had clogged the teeth so that they could no longer separate the cotton. Mr. Whitney looked puzzled.

Mrs. Greene picked up a brush from the hearth. "Why can't you use this?" she asked.

"It is the very thing," replied Mr. Whitney.

He then made a brush which turned against the cylinder and thus kept it clean and free of seeds. Then Mrs. Greene sent for her neighbors to see the gin work.

The planters were amazed at the simple machine. How easily it turned! How fast the snow white cotton came through the iron slits! Each was delighted and asked Mr. Whitney to make one for him. Then others came to see it, and soon the news brought men from a distance. But Mr. Whitney refused to let these strangers see his gin, because he had not yet got his patent, which would keep other people from stealing his idea.

Then some one broke into the shed where he kept his gin and stole it one night. This did not cause Mr. Whitney much worry, for he could easily make another. At last he sold enough gins to build a factory, but some one burned it just as it was finished. He tried to keep others from copying his machine, and this took him into court, where he lost all he had made. His patent lasted for fourteen years, and when that time had passed, thousands of gins were made, from which he got no money.

Whitney and the Cotton Gin

Eli Whitney made another invention for manufacturing guns which brought him plenty of money, but he received very little for his invention of the cotton gin. He will always be remembered because he helped his country by solving the problem of how to separate seed from cotton.

CHAPTER XXXV

QUICK-SILVER BOB BUILDS A STEAMBOAT

"What do you want with that quicksilver?" asked one of the workmen at the gun shop in Lancaster, Pennsylvania. "What are you up to now?"

Young Robert Fulton smiled as he replied, "I just want to make something with it."

"All right, Quick-Silver Bob," said the workman. "Show it to me when you finish." He liked this eager-eyed boy who came almost every day to watch the guns being made. He often drew pictures which the men put on the guns to make them sell more easily.

All the men were interested in the air gun which Robert made for himself. They liked the sturdy toys which he made and the fine lead pencils which were far better than any the men had seen.

One day he and his friend, Chris Gumpf, went fishing on the Conestoga Creek. Chris's father went with the boys. They got on a large flat-boat and used long poles to push it through the water. It was hard work to make the boat go where they wanted. It was hard to guide it down stream, but it was still harder to push the boat up stream.

"I am tired of poling this boat," said Quick-Silver Bob. "I am going to make a boat which will go without paddles or poles!"

Quick-Silver Bob's Steamboat

He first drew pictures of his boat. Then he made a model which looked like a toy. He carefully cut each piece of wood, and he made a paddle-wheel and put this in his model boat. Chris thought it would work, and he helped Robert build the larger one which would take them fishing. It took them some time to build the boat and the paddle wheel and the crank which turned it.

When the boat was finished and ready for the trial on the river, the boys were delighted to find that they could go up and down stream in their paddle-wheel boat. Each took turns at the crank while the other fished. No longer did they have to use poles!

When Robert Fulton was seventeen, he went to Philadelphia. There he earned his living by painting portraits and by drawing. In this way he earned enough money to buy a farm for his mother, where she and her other children could live.

Then he went to London, and did not come back to America for twenty years. He worked all that time trying to improve travel on rivers and canals; he also tried to invent submarines. At last he returned to America determined to make a steamboat that would improve travel on the rivers and canals of his own country.

Robert Fulton knew that no one believed a steamboat was going to take the place of sailboats which had been used for hundreds and hundreds of years. He had heard of John Fitch's steamboat and knew that no one would give money to help him with his work.

Robert Fulton determined to make a steamboat and

IN 1807 ROBERT FULTON'S STEAMBOAT, THE "CLERMONT," PUFFED ITS WAY UP THE HUDSON RIVER FROM NEW YORK TO ALBANY

prove that it was practical. He made several models before he tried to build his large steamboat of iron and wood. At last curious people flocked down to the Hudson River to see the strange looking ship which had not a single sail! Then the news was published that the "Clermont," Robert Fulton's steamboat, was going to Albany.

A great crowd of people began to gather early in the morning. These were in a merry mood. They laughed and joked at "Foolish Bob Fulton." Great clouds of black smoke began to rise from the stacks of the "Clermont."

Quick-Silver Bob's Steamboat

"Look!" shouted the crowd. The steamboat is on fire!" The boat's wheels began to turn slowly around.

"Is it moving yet?" asked someone.

"How can a boat move when there are neither sails nor oars?" scornfully replied another.

But the boat was moving! The smiles died away. A hush swept over the people. The boat was moving faster now and faster. More and more rapidly the paddle-wheel beat the water. The boat was gaining speed.

"Hurrah! Hurrah!" shouted the people, "Hurrah! Hurrah for Fulton!"

The "Clermont" sailed up the Hudson River to Albany. The men on the sailboats in the river were amazed at this boat which was pushed along by a steam engine and a paddle-wheel. The sound of the puffing engine and the flying sparks from the smoke-stack frightened many of the farmers who lived near the river banks.

The "Clermont" made the return trip from Albany to New York without any trouble. Robert Fulton had proved that the steamboat was practical and could go upstream as well as down in perfect safety. That was in 1807—two hundred years after the English came to Jamestown. In many ways our country was growing.

Two years after the first trip on the Hudson River, there were steamboats on other large rivers. They were also on many of the lakes. Soon the Mississippi and Ohio rivers were having fast steamboats, and the old fashioned flat-boats were slowly pushed aside and their places were taken by Robert Fulton's steamboats.

CHAPTER XXXVI

A FARMER BOY MAKES A REAPER

"It cuts, father, it cuts!" shouted the young man, Cyrus McCormick, as he ran along beside the clumsy reaper which his father built. "It cuts!" he cried joyfully to himself as he watched the long knives go down through the tall green wheat that May day on their farm near Lexington, Virginia.

Cyrus turned to look at the fallen wheat. He was shocked to see that it was tangled and torn, a mass of ruined straw! He was disappointed, and very sorry for his father. Robert McCormick, had failed again to make his reaper a success. Cyrus knew that his father's dream was to make a machine which would help the farmers harvest their wheat and save the back-breaking toil of cutting it by hand.

Cyrus was twenty-two years old, and he knew what hard work harvesting was. As a boy, he had often cut the grain with a small curved scythe. His back had ached from having to bend over. The muscles in his arms had cramped from the cutting, and blisters had hurt his hands.

When he grew older he had cut the tough grain with a cradle. This was only a larger scythe, which had long wooden fingers fastened to the back of the knife. These fingers caught the grain as it was cut, and then the men threw it out in little piles for the men and boys who came

A Farmer Boy Makes a Reaper

along later and bound it into bundles or shocks. Cyrus had tried to use a cradle when he was fifteen but he was too slight. He had then gone to his father's shop and made a smaller scythe.

Cyrus's father did not show how disappointed he was when he saw the ruined wheat.

"Will you try again, father?" asked Cyrus.

"No, son," replied Mr. McCormick. "I can do no more. I haven't the knives right and I do not know how to improve them!"

"Then I shall try," declared Cyrus. "I will have one ready by the time the wheat is ripe."

"In six weeks?" asked his father.

Cyrus went to the little blacksmith shop. He made a model of his machine and changed the kind of knife which his father used. Cyrus knew that if his machine was to be a useful one, it must work not only when the wheat was dry, but when the grain had been bent and beaten down by the storms.

The young man became so interested in his reaper that he worked at night, too. He carefully cut and fashioned each wooden piece. He heated and bent the few iron pieces which he needed. Jo Anderson, a colored slave, worked with Cyrus, side by side. Jo kept the bellows going. He held parts in place while Cyrus fastened them where they belonged. Hour after hour Jo helped Cyrus test each new part.

Robert McCormick was thrilled as he watched his son's determination. He was proud when he saw how

Those Who Dared

fast the machine took shape. He was sure his son would succeed. He gave him every encouragement.

And so did Cyrus's mother. She was a good gardener, and no doubt she often stopped her work among the flowers and stole into the little shop to find how the reaper was going.

There is not much to tell us about that very hot July day in 1831 when Jo hitched the horse to the reaper. No doubt Jo felt proud as he climbed upon the horse's back and started off. Fortunately for us there is a picture of this first machine.

Some of the McCormick neighbors came to see the reaper work. Colonel James McDowell and Captain William Massie were most interested in the machine, next to Cyrus's own family. Both of these men had watched the boy make his reaper.

Cyrus walked along beside the reaper as Jo drove the horse which pulled it through the grain. When he saw it cut through the tall swaying golden wheat, he knew that he had succeeded. It cut six acres of wheat before dark. This was more than several men could have done in one day with the old-fashioned cradles. His reaper was good. He would keep on until it was better.

The farmers were delighted. Yet they were not willing to buy one.

"It is too fang-dangle," said one old farmer. "It will get out of gear."

"Yes," agreed his friend, "I'll just stick to my cradle. I know that will work."

CYRUS MCCORMICK'S REAPER

The next year Cyrus made improvements in his reaper and gave some exhibitions of the way it worked, near Lexington, Virginia. But he was still not satisfied with it. He did not yet try to sell it. For several years he and his father manufactured iron instead of making reapers. Then, almost ten years, after that day when he and Jo showed what the reaper could do, he sold the first one. The next year he sold six; the next year, seven; the next year twenty-five; and the next year, fifty.

In the meanwhile, many of his friends were going west. Cyrus heard glowing accounts of the rich farm lands in the Ohio country. Thousands of pioneers from the East were settling in the valleys beyond the Allegheny Moun-

Those Who Dared

tains. Cyrus decided to make a trip to the West. He was delighted with the wide open valleys, so different from those in Virginia. He wrote home, "Reapers are a luxury in Virginia, but a necessity in this western land of plains."

Cyrus felt the call to go west. He had faith in his reaper. He wanted to start a factory where the country was suited for raising all kinds of grain. He made plans and built his factory in the small city of Chicago. His brother went into business with him. The reaper could do the work of ten men. Cyrus saw a great future in wheat. That year he sold hundreds of reapers. He made only a small profit on each machine. He used the very best materials. His reapers were well built and strong.

Cyrus McCormick made friends, not only for himself but for his reapers. Once when there was a failure of crops in the Middle West, Cyrus went out to visit the farmers. Now the men could not pay for the machines as they had promised. "Do not worry," Mr. McCormick said to the anxious farmers as he shook hands with them. "I will trust you." This he did, and not one penny did he lose by them.

Mr. McCormick did not forget his colored friend, Jo Anderson. When Jo was too old to work any longer, Mr. McCormick gave him a home and all that Jo needed. During the rest of his life Mr. McCormick never stopped improving his machines. The McCormick reapers and other farm machinery were sold, not only in America, but in all the countries in the world where wheat is grown in large quantities.

A Farmer Boy Makes a Reaper

Mr. McCormick was generous to all those who were deserving. He gave money to schools and to worthy boys and girls who could not afford to pay for their education. He did much to make Chicago the huge business center that it is, and he also helped to build beauty into this city where he lived and reared his family.

CHAPTER XXXVII

THE TOM THUMB RACES WITH A HORSE CAR

On the Fourth of July in 1828 an old man, Charles Carroll, stuck a spade into the ground marking the beginning of a big event. Near by were many prominent business men watching him. They loved him dearly, for he had done much for his home in Maryland and had signed the Declaration of Independence, fifty-two years before. Though now an old, old man, he had vision. He had faith in the future of railroads. He was breaking ground for one of the first tracks on which a steam train would run in America.

"I consider this among the most important acts of my life," he said, "second only to signing the Declaration of Independence, if second to that."

The steam railroads were first used in England. When Philip Thomas of Baltimore was on a visit there, he saw they could be used where canals and stage-coaches could not. When he returned to Baltimore he decided to organize the Baltimore and Ohio Railroad and to build the tracks across the mountains. He heard that Peter Cooper of New York had built an engine which was so small that it looked like a boiler on the kitchen stove. The engine was no larger than a tiny work-car when it was completed. It was called the "Tom Thumb."

"THE ENGINE GAVE A PUFF AND THE HORSE GAVE A SNORT AND OFF THEY WENT SIDE BY SIDE"

It was an exciting time August 28, 1830, when the men tried it out on the Baltimore and Ohio tracks which had been laid from Baltimore for a distance of thirteen miles. Peter Cooper had an open car hitched on to the little engine. The men who were putting in their money to help build the railroad and some of their friends climbed into the car. The men were breathless. They were going so fast, fifteen miles an hour around curves! One man took out his pencil when he was told he was riding at eighteen miles an hour and wrote several sentences to show that he could write when going as fast as that.

Now the stage-coach companies made fun of the Tom Thumb. They determined to fight their rival. The Stage-Coach Company in Baltimore challenged the Tom Thumb to race with their horse-car on its return trip to

Those Who Dared

Baltimore. This could easily be done as two double tracks had been built. On September 18, 1830, a strong gray horse was hitched to the horse-car for the race.

One of those who rode on the Tom Thumb wrote that the engine gave a puff and the horse gave a snort and off they went side by side.

At first the horse had the best of it, for he did not have to wait for the steam to get up as did the Tom Thumb. So the horse got ahead.

Then the safety valve of the engine lifted and a thin blue smoke-like mist arose. The whistle sounded. The engine began to go faster and faster. The passengers shouted and cried as they gained nearer and nearer to the coach drawn by the gray horse. Then the Tom Thumb passed the horse.

"Hurrah!" cried the men. "Tom Thumb is winning!"

The driver struck the gray horse with his whip. He ran faster and faster, the foam spreading around his harness. He pulled and panted and it looked as if Tom Thumb had indeed won.

Then something went wrong with the Tom Thumb. There was a leak in the boiler. The safety valve no longer screamed, and the Tom Thumb, for want of breath, began to wheeze and pant. Mr. Cooper and his fireman cut their hands as they tried to stop the leak. Then the fire burned down too low to make enough steam.

"Here comes the horse-car!" cried the men. "It is gaining on us!"

Tom Thumb and the Horse Car

And indeed the gray horse not only gained on them but soon the horse-car passed the Tom Thumb.

Mr. Cooper stopped the leak and started the fire to burn. Off they went again but not fast enough to overtake the horse-car. Though Mr. Cooper lost that race, he had proved the Tom Thumb was a success and that a railroad was practical.

Stage-coaches were still used for years. But as railroads made more and more improvements, stage-coaches gradually disappeared.

CHAPTER XXXVIII

THE DOT AND DASH CODE CARRIES MESSAGES

Did you ever hold a small mirror in your hand and catch a bit of sunlight upon it? You can then throw the light into a window across the way, or into a shadowed spot. This is the way the Egyptians, thousands of years ago, signaled to their armies during a war. Indians signaled to their tribes by lighting fires. When they won a victory they could not telegraph or telephone the news as we do today. They had to send the news or messages by runners from village to village. Sometimes weeks and months passed before their people back home received the news.

This is the story of the boy who made it possible for messages to go quickly by telegraph. His name was Samuel Finley Breese Morse.

Slogans and mottoes were popular when Sam was a boy. He chose a good one for his motto. It was, "Do Something for Your Fellow man." Perhaps his father, who was a minister, helped him choose it.

Sam studied hard and went to Yale College when he was only fifteen years old. He was poor, like many other fine boys. He had to help earn the money which paid for his room and board. He did this by painting little pictures of his classmates for five dollars apiece.

The Dot and Dash Code

When he was graduated from college, he went to London, and there he studied art for four years. He won medals and made a name for himself, but he could not sell his pictures. At last he returned home. He found it even harder to make money in America.

Morse wanted to study art in France. He went abroad, but met failure again and sadly packed his paintings for the journey home.

He sailed on the ship "Sully." One day he met Dr. Charles Thomas Jackson on board the ship. Dr. Jackson showed him an electro-magnet which he had brought from London. Morse was deeply interested in it. As he watched the magnet work, an idea came to him. It was a plan for sending messages by electricity. He drew a picture of an electro-magnet with a rod at one end of it like a pencil. This rod or pencil was to make a dot or dash when the electricity was turned on. He drew a plan for the printing frame of the instrument.

When he left the "Sully" he said, "Well, Captain, should you hear of the telegraph one of these days as the wonder of the world, remember that the discovery was made on board the good ship 'Sully.'"

But Morse was still poor. Again he had to paint to make a living. There was no money with which to buy materials for his invention. He was appointed as a professor in the University of the City of New York. This gave him more time to work on his crude telegraph.

He needed money for wires, springs, and batteries. He decided to take his model to his friend, Professor Gale.

Those Who Dared

While he was there a young man came in. He watched Professor Morse explain his instrument. This young man was Alfred Vail. He was delighted with the new instrument. He asked questions.

"Are you going to develop it with a longer line?" asked Alfred Vail.

"I will as soon as I get the money," replied Morse.

"How much do you need?" asked Vail.

"It will take $2000," replied Professor Morse.

"If I get the $2000," asked Alfred Vail, "will you take me in as a partner?"

"Indeed I will," promised the Professor.

Alfred Vail hurried to his home in Morristown, New Jersey. He went straight to the Speedwell Iron Works, where his father was in charge. He told him of what he had seen, of the need for money and of his wish to become Professor Morse's partner.

Mr. Vail was delighted. He gave his son the money and Alfred hurried off to ask Morse to bring his invention down to show it to his father. Professor Morse was glad to go and show the instrument to Mr. Vail. The partners worked hard and faithfully until they had a better telegraph ready to try. The day was set. Mr. Morse was in New York; Alfred was in Morristown.

Alfred Vail spoke to his apprentice boy, "Run, William, and tell father to come. I am ready to telegraph to New York."

Mr. Vail came in. He wrote on a piece of paper these words, "A patient waiter is no loser."

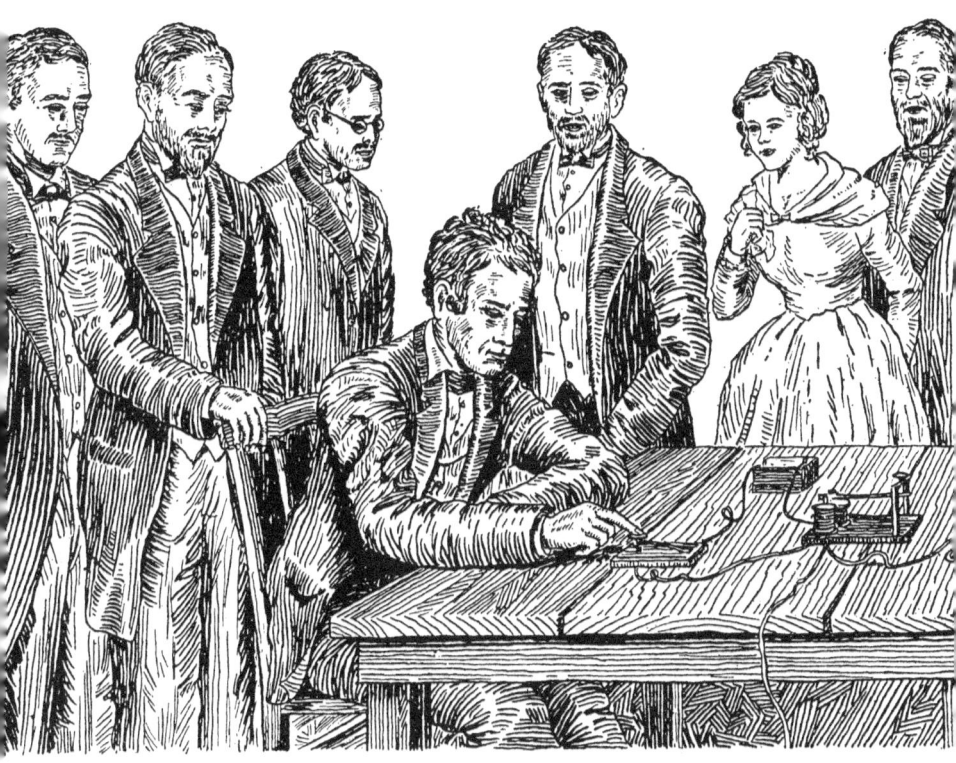

THE FIRST PUBLIC MESSAGE SENT OVER THE FIRST COMPLETED TELEGRAPH LINE FROM WASHINGTON TO BALTIMORE, ON MAY 24, 1844, WAS "WHAT HATH GOD WROUGHT"

He handed it to his son, saying, "If you can send that message to Morse by code and he can read it, I shall be convinced."

"Click, click—tap—tap," went the rod. Away it went over the wires to Professor Morse in New York. There he took the message, wrote it down and instantly read the words. His instrument was a success.

But once more troubles arose for the partners. They had patents to protect their invention, but they did not have money with which to put up a telegraph line. They could not go on with their work.

Those Who Dared

Then Professor Morse went to Washington. He lived in a tiny room and often went hungry. He talked to the men in the Senate, and he talked to others.

One day a senator said to him, "You need not stay here. The Senate is not in sympathy with your work. The senators are not interested. I advise you to go home and think no more about it!"

The poor inventor went back to his lonely room. He knelt down and prayed. It was far into the night before he went to sleep. He had paid his rent and board and now had only thirty-seven cents left.

The next morning, Annie Elliott, the daughter of one of his friends, called on him. She said, "Professor Morse, I have come to congratulate you!"

"To congratulate me?" asked the astonished Professor. "On what?"

"Why on the passage of your bill in the Senate," replied Miss Elliott.

The inventor was delighted. The Senate had passed the bill the night before.

"You shall send the first message over the wire," Professor Morse promised her. When the poles had been put up and the wires strung, Professor Morse did not forget. He asked Annie for the message, and this is what went over the first telegraph line on a May morning in 1844, "What Hath God Wrought!"

Professor Morse had lived up to his motto. His work was a service to his fellow man.

CHAPTER XXXIX

THE INDIA RUBBER MAN

"Can you tell me where I can find Mr. Charles Goodyear?" asked a stranger in New York.

"No," replied the man, "but you will know him when you see him."

"I am a stranger," said the first man. "How can I know one whom I have never seen."

"Oh," laughed the man, "Charles Goodyear will be dressed in an India rubber coat, an India rubber vest, and an India rubber hat. He will have an India rubber money purse without a cent of money in it. If it is raining he will be wearing India rubber shoes."

Whether this story is true or not, Charles Goodyear was called the India Rubber Man, and he did wear all these things which were made out of rubber. He and his father had been hardware merchants and manufacturers, but they had lost all their money. Charles knew that if he could find a way to keep rubber from sticking and melting in summer, it would make him and his father rich. So he worked hard to improve India rubber.

The India rubber trees grow, as you know, in those countries where it is very hot. The trees are gashed by men who catch the milk or liquid of the tree in buckets. Something is then put in, so that the rubber separates from the liquid and forms a soft mass.

TAPPING RUBBER TREES IN BRAZIL TO GET LATEX FROM WHICH RUBBER IS MADE. TAPPING IS DONE IN THE EARLY MORNING BEFORE THE SUN IS HOT ENOUGH TO CHECK THE FLOW OF LATEX. IT RUNS. DROP BY DROP, INTO THE CUPS FOR AN HOUR AFTER THE CUT HAS BEEN MADE

The Indians in South America made bottles out of rubber. They made heavy shoes from it, too. But it cost a great deal of money to buy rubber shoes from South America. Charles Goodyear knew how many American merchants had brought the rubber to the United States and had made shoes from it. But what queer shoes they were! They melted or grew too soft to wear when the weather was warm, and they were too stiff to wear in winter. The rubber rain-coats which were made in America were like the shoes. In winter the

The India Rubber Man

coats were hard and stiff, while in summer they became sticky and soft.

That is why Charles Goodyear kept on trying to make rubber vests, coats, caps, and other things. His friends laughed at him and teased him when he made a rubber cane. Then he made rubber so thin it was like paper and he wrote on it. He even made a door-plate of rubber.

Charles Goodyear spent all the money he could get to buy more rubber. His family often went without food in order that he might buy rubber to try out his ideas. His friends had to help him by giving him money to buy coal and wood. Some say he even sold his children's school books in order to buy rubber.

One day Charles Goodyear mixed some sulphur with the rubber. It was very cold, and he went over and stood by the stove which was almost red-hot. Some of the mixture fell on the stove. Charles looked in amazement at the ball of rubber and sulphur. It did not melt and run all over the stove. When he took it off it looked and felt like a piece of soft leather. This was just what he had been trying to get. But he must test his "vulcanized" rubber still further. It was freezing cold outdoors. He took his ball of rubber and nailed it to the door outside. If it did not freeze and turn hard he knew he had found the secret for making rubber useful. The next morning he was delighted to find the rubber was just as he had put it out the night before.

Then Charles Goodyear began the long task of getting the right amount of sulphur to mix with his rubber. He

Those Who Dared

at last made some business men realize that there was money in his discovery. They built a factory for him to make rubber coats, shoes, cloth, and many other useful things. Now when you ride in automobiles whose tires are called "Goodyear," you know that they are so named in honor of the man who was called the India Rubber Man.

THE LIBRARY

Stories in Other Books

"How Eli Whitney Invented the Cotton Gin," "Robert Fulton And The Steamboat," "The Coming of the Steam Railroad," "The Building of the Erie Canal," "The Invention of the Telegraph," in *Makers of the Nation*, by Fanny E. Coe.

"Southward to the Land of Cotton," in *Then and Now in Dixie*, by Rose Mortimer Ellzey MacDonald.

"Connecting the West with the East," in *These United States and How They Came to Be*, by Gertrude Hartman.

"Samuel Morse And The Telegraph," in *Our Country Past and Present*, by William Lewis Nida and Victor L. Webb.

"Inventions and Discoveries Change American Life," in *Our Nation Grows Up*, by Eugene C. Barker.

"Travel in Virginia," "Mountain Boys Who Made Machines," in *The Story of Virginia*, by Carrie Hunter Willis and Lucy S. Saunders.

From Trail to Railway Through the Appalachians, by Albert Perry Brigham.

"The Railway-Train," in *How the World Rides*, by Florence Cornelia Fox.

SELF-TESTING GAME

This is another matching game. On a sheet of paper write the names in Column I. After each name write the event

Something New

found in Column II which tells something about this person. Each name correctly matched counts 3.

I	II
Samuel Slater	made a Tom Thumb engine.
Eli Whitney	invented the telegraph.
Cyrus McCormick	made a weaving mill from memory.
Robert Fulton	invented the reaper.
Peter Cooper	discovered how to vulcanize rubber.
Samuel Morse	invented the cotton gin.
Charles Goodyear	built the first successful steamboat.

Count your score. Did you make 21, the highest possible score?

Choose Something to Do

1. Make a list of the pleasures and helps in living now in your home which you would not have if there had been no inventions since the days of George Washington.

2. Make three-minute speeches on one of the following subjects:
    a. The Tom Thumb Races with the Horse Car
    b. A Country Boy Invents a Reaper
    c. Morse Gets Help at the Last Moment

3. Perhaps some members of the class would like to make models of a sailboat and a paddle-wheel steamboat.

4. Make and tell to your class a story such as a boy would have told when he reached home: after seeing the "Clermont" on her first trip up the Hudson; or after seeing the race between the Tom Thumb and the horse car.

PART IX

OUR COUNTRY REACHES FROM COAST TO COAST

CHAPTER XL

THE OREGON TRAIL IS OPENED

How should you like to drive in a wagon, across prairies and over mountains, where there are no roads at all? Over a hundred years ago, Marcus Whitman, a young man from New York, did so.

One day young Whitman read a strange story in his church paper. It told how four Indian chiefs rode their lean wiry ponies into the post at St. Louis. The ponies were thirsty, hungry, and tired. Their riders were, too. Their soft embroidered doe-skin clothes and their long black hair were covered with dust.

They were taken to meet General Clark, who was the Indian agent in St. Louis. General Clark treated the Indians kindly and won their confidence. They told him why they had traveled "many, many moons all summer and fall," from their home in the Oregon country. They heard that the "Pale Faces" had a wonderful Book of Life. Their people wanted one, too, and they had come to get it. The "Book of Life" was the Bible.

The chiefs spent the winter at the Post. Everyone liked them. When the grass grew green in the spring, the chiefs prepared to return home. General Clark gave them a farewell dinner. There were presents for the Indians. At the end of the dinner General Clark asked the Indians to make a speech.

FOUR INDIAN CHIEFS FROM THE OREGON COUNTRY RIDE INTO THE ARMY POST AT ST. LOUIS TO ASK THE PALE FACES FOR THEIR "BOOK OF LIFE," THE BIBLE

What a picture the oldest chief made as he rose to his full height! He folded his arms across his breast and held his head high. His hair held a bright feather, and he still wore his quill-embroidered clothes. He spoke in his own language which, if it were translated into English, would be something like this:

"I have come over many trails from the land of the Setting Sun. I come for my people who are blind and sit in darkness. My own eye is only partly open. Now I go back with both eyes shut. I braved many dangers to come to you who are friends of my people. I go

The Oregon Trail

back with both arms empty and broken. You make my feet heavy with gifts, and my moccasins will grow old taking them home; yet the Book of Life is not among them. How can I go back to my people? They will die in darkness. They will not find the path to your hunting ground. They will go to some other man's hunting ground, for they have no white man to go with them. I say no more!" Young Whitman read all this in his church paper, and then the paper asked the question, "Who will go beyond the Rocky Mountains and carry the Book of Life?"

Marcus Whitman determined to take the Bible to the Indians. He came of brave people. His own mother had walked four hundred miles with a baby in her arms when his father had decided to "go west" from New England to New York.

Marcus asked his church to send him as a preacher to Oregon. He won the permission of the church, and then went west to see the country. When he returned he was more than ever determined to go, but he decided to marry his sweetheart before he left again for the west coast.

Most of the trip to St. Louis was made by boat over canals and down the Ohio River. In St. Louis Mr. and Mrs. Whitman were joined by Dr. and Mrs. Spalding. The four young people took a steamboat up the Missouri River to the Council Bluff. There were of course no trains going across the prairies in those days. "We do not mind driving across the plains," declared Marcus

WHEN MARCUS WHITMAN STARTED WEST FROM HIS HOME IN THE STATE OF NEW YORK, A PART OF HIS JOURNEY WAS ON THE ERIE CANAL, ONE OF THE HIGHWAYS TO THE WEST IN THE EARLY DAYS

Whitman. So they bought a wagon and a pair of stout mules.

There were dangers all along the way, but these young people sang and kept up a steady cheerful talk. At last they reached Fort Hill, a post of the American Fur Trading Company. The officers there discouraged them by telling of the loneliness of the country, of the dangers of unfriendly Indians, and of wild animals. The officers showed the young people the broken-down wagons and farming implements of other men who had come out to settle and had all gone back home. These men did not want their trading country to be settled because settlements would spoil their rich fur trading business.

But the young people were not afraid. They went on. When they came to the steep mountains, where

The Oregon Trail

there were huge rocks, their wagon rolled and bumped along and stood the strain. They crossed deep, swiftly flowing streams and rivers. Twice the little wagon was overturned and some of their supplies were lost or ruined by the water. Once it rolled down the deep cliff of the mountain and two wheels were broken beyond repair. It was a sad and dilapidated wagon which finally rolled into Fort Walla Walla. After seven months of traveling, all the paint was gone and the spokes were broken, but it was the first wagon to enter the Oregon country.

The Indians had heard of their coming. There were hundreds waiting to welcome them and the Book of Life.

The Oregon country at this time, though claimed by both England and America, did not belong to either country. The missionaries wished this country to belong to America, but the men in Congress did not seem to want it.

"I will go myself to Washington," declared Marcus Whitman. "I will do what I can to save Oregon for the nation." His friend, General Lovejoy, went with Whitman. What a terrible journey they had! They asked a guide to go with them, for it was winter and the ground was covered with snow. The three set off on horseback. They were in several blizzards. Their guide deserted them. They lost their way and their food. Their horses had no corn or hay. They crossed icy streams and many times had to stop and build fires to thaw out their clothes which were drenched in the crossing. Wild animals

Those Who Dared

howled at their camps at night and stole whatever they left outside. After five months Whitman at last reached Washington.

Though dressed like a pioneer, he stood before President Tyler and Secretary Daniel Webster and answered every argument anyone raised against having Oregon belong to the United States. President Tyler agreed not to decide the Oregon question until settlers could go into the Oregon country.

How happy Marcus Whitman was! General Lovejoy spread the news over the frontier that in the spring he and Marcus Whitman would lead a band of settlers into the Oregon country. They started from a place near where Kansas City now stands, making a trail which came to be known as the Oregon Trail, over which thousands went later to the Pacific Coast.

CHAPTER XLI

GOLD! GOLD! THE LAND OF GOLD!

Land of Gold! The Spaniards' dream of finding gold, as you remember, led them to America. Many of them became rich trading with the Indians. Some of these went up into California, the Land of Sunshine. There they built trading stations. They also built missions for teaching the Indians religion.

A few American hunters and trappers also found their way to California.

When this section was a part of Mexico, John Sutter asked the Mexican government to give him a grant of land in the lovely Sacramento Valley. Mexico agreed to grant him the land if Mr. Sutter would be its agent or governor over the Indians and Mexicans who lived there. This Mr. Sutter said he would do, and a large fort was built on his huge ranch. From this time on, he was called Captain Sutter, and his ranch was called the Fort.

More and more Americans came to California. There was a real need for lumber with which to build houses.

Captain Sutter was a good business man. He decided to build a sawmill fifty miles up in the mountains. He called in Mr. Marshall, a carpenter from New Jersey, who had built some houses for him, and told him his plan.

Those Who Dared

"The river will turn our mill," said Captain Sutter. "Then we can float the lumber down the river to the places where there is need for it. I want you to buy the sawmill, hire the men, and get the lumber out."

Marshall lost no time in getting the sawmill and hiring six white men and twelve Indians. While the white men built a dam, the Indians cut the trees. They dug a ditch called a race for the water to run through and over the great mill wheel.

The water was turned loose over the dam, the great wheel turned, and everything went smoothly. But Marshall decided there was not enough water coming through the race. He cut off the water and soon there was none in the race ditch. "It must be dug wider," thought Marshall. Just then he saw glistening in the late afternoon light, some bright bits of yellow gravel. He looked to see if any of the men were near. But all were in the camp eating their supper. Mr. Marshall stooped down and picked up some gravel and slipped it into his pocket.

Marshall did not tell any of the men what he suspected —that his pieces of gravel were gold! Early the next morning he saddled his pony and rode down to the Fort.

When Captain Sutter saw his partner he called, "What is up, Marshall? What is on your mind?"

"Come into your office," replied his partner. Then he turned his pocket inside out and let the yellow gravel fall on the table.

"I found that in the mill race," he said. "What do you think it is?"

The Land of Gold

"It looks like gold," replied the astonished Captain. "But you know many others have been fooled with yellow clay and rocks. I have read a book on gold, Marshall. It says if it is gold, an acid will not tarnish it or eat it up. I have some acid here. Let us try it on this gravel of yours."

The men held their breath as they poured the acid on the yellow gravel. They could not believe their own eyes, as the gold became clean and remained glistening as it had been before being tested. They tried again and again, and each time the gold was left shining clear.

"We had better not tell anyone about this," said Marshall. "We had better stick to our sawmill business for there is gold in that now. We cannot tell how soon the vein of gold would give out."

But Marshall could not keep his secret. Other workmen found bits of the precious metal along the sides of the mill race, too.

The cook at the camp was Mrs. Wimmer. She used her odd scraps of meat and grease and made soap with them. The scraps were put into a big iron pot, lye was added, with a little water, and all was boiled until it got thick.

The men thought of dropping some of their tiny yellow bits of gravel down into the boiling soap. If the lye did not eat or tarnish it, they would know it was gold.

How eagerly and impatiently the men watched that pot of soap boil and waited for it to cool! They hardly gave Mrs. Wimmer time to get her soap out of the pot

"PANNING" GOLD IN CALIFORNIA. THE GOLD-BEARING SAND WAS PUT IN A PAN OF WATER AND THE HEAVY PARTICLES OF GOLD SANK TO THE BOTTOM. THE SAND WAS THEN POURED OFF AND THE GOLD REMAINED

the next morning. Imagine their delight and their wild shouts when they saw the tiny yellow bits of gold as bright and shining as they had been when they were dropped into the boiling pot!

Off went the men to find axes, pans with which to wash the gravel free from dirt, picks with which to dig the gravel from the river bank! No more wood-cutting or building of dams for them. Over night they had become miners who made as much as $25 and $50 a day.

The news traveled fast, and all along the fifty miles to the Fort went the magic words, "Gold up in the moun-

The Land of Gold

tains near the sawmill." The whisper spread to San Francisco and eastward across the plains to the Mississippi River and to the East beyond.

"Gold in California!" became the cry which made men everywhere drop whatever they were doing and rush for the "Diggings" as the Camp was now called.

Doctors left their patients. Lawyers left the courts. Merchants left their shops. Farmers left their ranches. All rushed to buy picks, axes, and other supplies. They, too, became miners, and their leather pouches were soon filled with the golden nuggets.

Some men hastily put up hotels, dance halls, and gambling parlors in San Francisco. Soon the miners were tramping back to the city to spend their gold nuggets.

CHAPTER XLII

THE FORTY-NINERS AND HOW THEY TRAVELED

After the news of the discovery of gold in 1848 reached the East, the newspapers printed such headlines as this, "Land of Gold Discovered."

The next year thousands of people flocked west to become rich by digging gold. These were called the "Forty-Niners." Many of them took their wives and children with them. Some chose the Oregon Trail for a part of the way and then turned south and west, traveling through what is now Nevada and Utah.

Soon there was a steady stream of wagons being drawn by great heavy horses, four or six to each wagon. There were heavy two-wheeled creaking carts, pulled by mules or oxen. These were passed by gayly painted wagons, built like a boat, called prairie schooners, which had heavy white canvas tops, like a hood, and were fitted up inside with kitchen utensils, household furniture, and cots on which the family slept.

The travelers were joined by others whom they overtook or met along the way. Thus quite a party would be formed. This was done for protection from Indians or robbers along the lonely trails.

These Forty-Niners were brave and sturdy. They did not fear the storms of the desert, or the sweeping winds

STAGE-COACH TRAVEL IN THE WEST IN THE GOLD RUSH DAYS

which blinded their eyes and sifted sand and dust into everything they ate and into the folds of their blankets and clothes. They cheerfully went without water and gave it to others when they could not find a spring or a stream. Sometimes they died from thirst. Some could not stand the steady strain of traveling over the rough roads, and the fierce heat of the desert killed others. Soon there were little stakes pointing to the graves of those who died on the way.

The boys and girls stood the trip better than the older people. The boys helped to drive the mules, led pack horses, cut fire wood, and pitched tents for the campers at night.

At last the weary gold seekers climbed the rocky sides

Those Who Dared

of the Sierra Mountains. They were tired, sore, and dusty. Often their clothing was in rags when they at last reached California.

While these people were traveling in their wagons, some of the neighbors were on the way to California by sea. They went in large rounded boats with low-swung sails. They sailed in any kind of boat which was considered at all safe. Down the Atlantic, around Cape Horn, and up into the Pacific to California they went.

The "Eliza" sailed from Salem, Massachusetts, with many young Forty-Niners aboard. They were very gay and in high spirits, for we are told that they made up new words to the popular song "Oh, Suzanna," and this is how their song went:

> I come from Salem City
> With a washbowl on my knee;
> I'm going to Cal-i-for-ni-a,
> The gold dust for to see.
>
> It rained all night the day I left,
> The weather it was dry
> The sun so hot I froze to death
> Susanna, don't you cry.
>
> Oh, Susanna!
> Oh, don't you cry for me!
> For I'm going to Cal-i-for-ni-a
> With a washbowl on my knee, etc.

THE "FLYING CLOUD," A FAMOUS CLIPPER SHIP THAT SAILED AROUND CAPE HORN, CARRYING PASSENGERS FROM NEW YORK TO SAN FRANSCISCO IN GOLD RUSH DAYS. IT CUT THE TIME FROM OVER 200 DAYS TO 89 DAYS

Those Who Dared

This tune became the song of the Forty-Niners and someone has said there are almost as many verses to the song as there were miners.

"Build faster boats!" complained the travelers, for it took from six months to a year to go by boat to California.

"Give us a quicker passage around the Horn!" the miners asked of the ship builders in Boston and Philadelphia.

Mr. Donald McKay was the first ship builder to meet these demands. He changed the almost round-shaped bows into long slender ones. These longer boats could cut through the waters more swiftly. They were called clipper ships. The masts were taller, and the Yankee clippers like the "Flying Cloud" took many men to this newly found land of gold in California.

When a party was ready to sail, there was a holiday. Old people and young people came to the port to see the ship start on its long journey. Wives, sweethearts, and mothers smiled bravely, though many of them turned aside to wipe away a tear as they realized how soon their loved ones would be leaving for California. The sailors went on board first and tugged at the mast ropes, and as they lifted the great heavy anchors they sang:

> A bully ship and a bully crew,
> Doo- da- doo- da!
> A bully mate and a captain too,
> Doo- da, doo- da- day!

The Forty-Niners
Then blow ye winds, heigh- ho,
For Cali-for-ny O!
There's plenty of gold,
So I've been told
On the banks of the Sacramento!

How seasick some of the men were! How tired all got of eating only dried salted meats, hard-tack, and fresh fish. They welcomed the first glimpse of California. They poured into San Francisco and bought supplies and were off for the Gold Diggings. There they spent the nights in the villages or shanties called the Red Dog, the Poker Flats, or some similar name.

Of course some of the Forty-Niners were not good men. They were rough, and many were not honest. Some of them drank too much whiskey and did many foolish things, like shooting out the lights in a dance hall. Some of the men were robbers and stole the gold for which others had worked. There were no jails, courts, or policemen.

Every man carried his own pistol. There were street fights, and men were often shot to death over some trifling quarrel.

Some of the men who loved law and peace talked over the terrible state of affairs. They made some simple rules or laws for the good of all and gave themselves power to punish anyone who broke the laws. These men were called "Watchers" because they watched for the safety of the people.

A WESTERN BOOM TOWN IN "THE DAYS OF OLD, AND THE DAYS OF GOLD, AND THE DAYS OF 'FORTY-NINE"

As gold grew scarcer and the miners made less, some of them began to see the rich country for the first time. Many had come to California just to get gold, never thinking of making a home there. Now some of the Forty-Niners decided to live along the coast. Many of them set out orange groves. Apricots and prunes were planted, as well as all kinds of vegetables. Grapes grew easily, and hundreds of acres were planted. Soon these crops brought in more gold than all the gold that had been mined!

CHAPTER XLIII

THE PONY EXPRESS

One of the greatest hardships of the Forty-Niners was leaving their old homes and not being able to hear from their loved ones and friends for months at a time. What a rush there was when a boat came into port! The men rushed to the little wooden post office. They were impatient while the postmaster sorted the letters into the many different piles—all the names beginning with A, then the names beginning with B, and so on down the alphabet. Sometimes it took him two days to sort all the letters. Long lines of men formed early in the morning and waited their turn to get to the window. Sometimes a man stepped out and another man took his place. This meant that one paid the other for his place in line to let him get closer to the window. One man paid as much as twenty-five dollars to get nearer to the post office window. The line often reached the entire length of the street. There the people stood for hours and hours. Men and women walked up and down the line and sold meat, bread, and hot coffee.

We have seen that the cry for faster boats brought better ones, and now the cry for faster travel and mail brought the stage-coaches from the Missouri River, run by regular companies back and forth to California. These were large vehicles with curving bottoms and sides.

THE FORTY-NINERS WAITING FOR LETTERS FROM HOME

There were seats for nine passengers inside the coach, while two more could ride in front with the driver. From four to eight heavy horses pulled the wagon-like stage-coach. Its side curtains of heavy leather flapped in the wind when it rained or was cold. It took twenty days to go from the Missouri River to California. The driver also stored away the heavy leather sacks in which were letters for the Forty-Niners or for the people "back home."

The stage-coaches were often attacked by Indians, but the greatest danger to the travelers was not always from

The Pony Express

the Indians. The worst terror of the trip came from the white robbers. These robbers hid behind bushes or huge rocks in the bend of the narrow rough road. As the coach came around the curve, the men dashed out and caught hold of the reins. Others commanded the driver to get down at the point of a gun. Passengers were ordered to hold up their hands while the robbers took their money and jewels and stole what they wanted out of their bags. Sometimes a brave driver shot the leading robber and raced his horses until he got away.

To meet the demand for faster mail, companies were formed. They knew that one man on a fast horse could travel more swiftly than the heavy stage-coaches. They decided to put men on fast ponies and send the mail by them. This was called the Pony Express.

One spring day the Pony Express was to start. The people came in to St. Joseph, Missouri, by the hundreds, for it was like a holiday. Every man shut up his store or shop. Flags floated along the main street, and the band played. A thrill of excitement swept the crowd as a little black pony was led from the Pike's Peak Livery Stable. The pony felt the excitement, too, for he switched his tail and stamped his strong, little hoofs.

Johnny Frey, twenty years old, handsome in his coat and spurred boots, with a broad red sash around his waist, awaited the signal to start. A cannon was fired. Off galloped Johnny to the post office. He was handed a leather mail-pouch in which were forty-nine letters and ten telegrams for the Californians.

THE PONY EXPRESS RIDER, "THE FLEET MESSENGER WHO SPED ACROSS THE CONTINENT FROM ST. JOSEPH, MISSOURI, TO SACRAMENTO, CARRYING LETTERS NINETEEN HUNDRED MILES IN EIGHT DAYS! ... THE PONY RIDER WAS USUALLY A LITTLE BIT OF A MAN BRIMFUL OF SPIRIT AND ENDURANCE. ... HE RODE A SPLENDID HORSE THAT WAS BORN FOR A RACER AND FED AND LODGED LIKE A GENTLEMAN"

"Get up," called Johnny to his pony. He waved his hat to the friends who called out, "Good luck, Johnny!" and "Don't let the Indians scalp you." But Johnny couldn't hear their cries because of the shouts of the people and the rush of the wind as it whistled through his hair!

At the same time another boy was leaving Sacramento.

The Pony Express

His name was Harry Roff. The letters in his pouch had been brought by steamer from San Francisco, and, besides these, he carried letters from Sacramento and the country near by. He too was honored by bands playing, flags flying, and calls of good wishes. On his bridle were two small American flags which fluttered about his pony's ears.

The Pony Express Company had built tiny stations along the road about twenty-five miles apart. Men were hired to keep these stations and to have a fresh horse ready for the rider when he came in. We can imagine how glad these lonely men were to have the riders come into their stations.

There were eighty young riders for the Pony Express. They were chosen for their honesty, bravery, and endurance. They were also picked according to their weight, for the horses could carry only so many pounds. The riders sometimes rode seventy-five miles a day. The letters had to be written on very thin paper, tied into neat bundles, and wrapped in oiled silk before being put into the pouches. The riders could take only twenty pounds of mail at a time. The mail was then sealed, and the pouches were strapped to the saddles. The company charged five dollars in advance for every letter sent from the East to California and the same price for a return trip.

Through the burning heat of the summer and through the blizzards of winter, the riders kept up their mail trips and mostly on schedule time. Often large sums of money were sent by the Pony Express. There was

WHEN YOUNG WILLIAM CODY (BUFFALO BILL) WAS A PONY EXPRESS RIDER, HE WAS ATTACKED BY INDIANS, BUT HE OUTRODE THEM

always danger of being held up, just as the stage-coaches were. One young rider named William Cody, afterward famous as Buffalo Bill, was given a large sum of money to carry to his station fifty miles away. He had always lived in the West and he knew how to use his head. He asked for an extra mail pouch. This he filled with carefully folded scrap paper.

The Pony Express

When the time came for him to start, Bill strapped the pouch with the scrap paper to his saddle. He carefully took the pouch which held the real money and hid that under his saddle blanket.

As he expected, some men came out in front of him as he rounded a curve, and stood in the middle of the narrow trail. Bill saw the pistols in their hands as one of them cried:

"Hands up, Bill. We know you and what you carry!"

"I carry the Express and it's hanging for you if you interfere with me," replied the bold young rider.

"Well, we don't want you," said the robber. "We want what you carry!"

"It won't do you any good to get this mail pouch," Bill told them, "for there is nothing valuable in it!"

"We'll be the judge of that, Bill" laughed the robber. "Throw us the bag or take a bullet. Which do you want, Bill?"

Buffalo Bill unfastened the fake pouch in which were folded scraps of paper and threw it to the men saying,

"If you will have it, take it."

The men rushed to pick up the fallen pouch. Bill spurred his pony and off he galloped past them and on out of danger before the robbers realized how they had been fooled.

Another time Bill Cody was attacked by Indians who were also on fast ponies. He fired several times as he galloped and so gained a running start. He managed to out-run them, and he reached his station safely.

Those Who Dared

The Pony Express carried the mail for almost two years. Then the Pacific Telegraph came. It no longer paid to keep the Express going. The nation owes these riders of the Pony Express a debt of gratitude, for they made the men and women more contented in their faraway new homes. They helped to unite the country when it first stretched from coast to coast.

THE LIBRARY
Stories in Other Books

"On to Oregon!" "Gold! Gold!! Gold!!!" *These United States and How They Came to Be,* by Gertrude Hartman.

"The Gold-Rush to California," "The Pony Express," in *Our Country Past and Present,* by William Lewis Nida and Victor L. Webb.

"Buried Treasure, Finding Gold in California," in *Great Moments in Exploration,* by Marion Florence Lansing.

"Scenes on the Oregon Trail," "The Settlement of California," in *Our Nation Grows Up,* by Eugene C. Barker.

SELF-TESTING GAMES
Game I

This is a completion game. On your paper write in a column the numbers 1 to 10. After each number write the word or words that make true the sentence having the same number. Each correct sentence counts 2.

1. Marcus Whitman went to the Oregon Country to take the ―― to the Indians.
2. Whitman wanted Oregon to belong to the ―― ――.
3. He and General Lovejoy opened the ―― ―― over which thousands later went to the Pacific Coast.
4. Mr. Marshall found gold in ―― while digging a mill dam.

From Coast to Coast

5. —— —— and Mr. Marshall were partners.
6. People from all parts of the country flocked to ——.
7. Some went by water around —— ——; others traveled by land over the —— —— and other routes.
8. To give faster travel to California, —— —— were used.
9. During the days of the Pony Express —— —— was one of the most daring riders.
10. When —— lines were opened to California, the Pony Express was no longer needed.

Count your score. Did you make 20, the highest possible score?

Game II

This is a game of dates. Connect the dates in Column B with the right events in Column A. On a sheet of paper write the events and dates in the order in which the dates are given. Each date correctly placed counts 3. Perhaps you will wish to look back in your book to get these dates just right.

A

1. The Declaration of Independence was signed
2. Plymouth was settled
3. Columbus discovered America
4. Jamestown was settled
5. The first successful steamboat sailed up the Hudson
6. Washington became our first president
7. Cornwallis surrendered at Yorktown
8. The Tom Thumb engine raced with the horse car
9. The first telegraph message was sent
10. Gold was discovered in California

B

October 12, 1492
in 1607
in 1620
July 4, 1776

Those Who Dared

October 19, 1781
April 30, 1789
in 1807
in 1830
in 1844
in 1848

The highest possible score is 30. What is your score?

Choose Something to Do

1. Draw pictures showing the following scenes:
   a. Marcus Whitman Dressed as a Pioneer Standing before the President
   b. A Scene on the Oregon Trail

2. Divide your class into two groups. Let one give a two-act play made around the subject "Gold Found in California"; the other, a two-act play around "The Pony Express." In the latter, two good scenes are "The Pony Express Starts from St. Joseph" and "Buffalo Bill Outwits the Robbers."

3. Look at the map in the back of this book. Let different members of the class choose different states or regions, and then have a "story relay race," one telling the story of Raleigh's colony; the next the story of the Jamestown, and so on, until the Pacific Ocean is reached.

INDEX

ACTIVITIES. *See* Something to Do.
Adams, Abby, daughter of John and Abigail Adams, childhood of, 109 ff.
Adams, Abigail, wife of John Adams and mother of John Quincy Adams, 109 ff.
Adams, John, father of John Quincy Adams and 2nd president of the U. S., 109 ff.; at First Continental Congress, 115 ff.; at Second Continental Congress, 147 ff.; signs Declaration of Independence, 152; in France, 163
Adams, John Quincy, son of John Adams and 6th president of the U. S., boyhood of, 109 ff.
Adams, Samuel, at Second Continental Congress, 147 ff.
Alamo, the, 233 ff.
Alexandria, Virginia, 107.
Allegheny Mountains, 257.
America, discovery of, 12 ff.
American Revolution, 147 ff., 154 ff., 164 ff., 172 ff.
Amsterdam, Holland, 60, 63, 65.
Anderson, Dr., donor of monument in St. Augustine, 23.
Anderson, Jo, colored man who helped Cyrus McCormick, 255 ff.
"Anne," Oglethorpe's ship, 86-87.
Architecture. *See* Homes.
Arkansas, 230.
Arkwright, Richard, inventor of the spinning jenny, 241.
Arnold, Benedict, 173.
Austin, Moses, father of Stephen F. Austin, plans colonization of Texas, 229-30.
Austin, Stephen F., boyhood and education of, 229; carries on his father's work of colonizing Texas, 230 ff.; settlement of in Texas, 231; pleads with Mexican government for the Texans, 232; imprisoned in Mexico City, 232; leads Texan fight for independence, 232; called "Father of Texas," 232.
Austin, Texas, 232.

BALTIMORE, Stage - Coach Company of, challenges the "Tom Thumb," 261
Baltimore and Ohio Railroad, started, 260-61
Barcelona, reception of Columbus in, 17
Baskets, made by Indians, 99
Battle of Lexington and Concord, 147
"Beaver," steamboat used by Stephen F. Austin, 230
Belvoir, home of the Fairfaxes, 107
Big Lick, 137
Bingham, Mrs., 189
Blockhouses, at Boonesboro, 138, 140
Boom town, a, 294
Boone, Daniel, boyhood of, 123-25; goes to North Carolina, 125-26; in French and Indian War, 127; marries Rebecca Bryan, 129, cabin of, 129-30; dress of, 130; meets John Finley, 132; goes west to hunt, 134-36; blazes the Wilderness Road, 137; and fort at Boonesboro, 137; rescues captured girls, 140-41; goes to Missouri, 142; old age of, 142-43; sees Lewis and Clark Expedition, 196

Index

Boone, Jemima, daughter of Daniel Boone, 139
Boonesboro, frontier fort, 137 ff.
Boston, and the Revolution, 116
Boston Harbor, closing of by British, 116
Boucher, Mr., tutor of Jack Custis, 105; the Washingtons visit, 105 ff.
Braddock, General, 127-28
Braintree, Massachusetts, home of the Adams family, 109 ff.
Brazos River, 230
Bridges, in early America, 192-93
Brooms, made by Indians, 99
Bryan, Rebecca, married Daniel Boone, 129 ff.
Buffalo Bill. *See* Cody, William.

CADE, KIN, a famous hunter, 224
Calloway, Betsy and Fanny, 139
Calvert, Colonel, of Maryland, 107
Calvert, Eleanor, bride of Jack Custis, 107, 108
Canal travel, 280
Cape Charles, 44
Cape Cod, 33
Cape Henry, 44
Carpenters' Hall, Philadelphia, 116, 152
Carroll, Charles, signs Declaration of Independence, 114; on July 4, 1828, breaks ground for first steam railroad in America, 260
Carson, Christopher (Kit), as a boy in Franklin, Mo., 221; runs away and joins caravan on Santa Fé Trail, 222-23; in Santa Fé, 223-24; meets Kin Cade, 224; learns trapping, 224-26; guides Frémont, 227-28
Carver, John, 57
Castell, Robert, Oglethorpe's friend, in Fleet Prison, 83 ff.
Catholics, at Continental Congress, 116
Charleston, S. C., receives Oglethorpe, 87; welcomes Lafayette, 172
Chesapeake Bay, 47
Chicago, McCormick factories in, 258-59
Chickahominy River, 47
China, trade with, 6, 15, 61, 63
Christian, Mr., dancing master, 105
City Tavern, Philadelphia, 116, 118
Claiborne, Governor, and the pirates, 208 ff.
Clark, George Rogers, a pioneer in Kentucky, 165; captures Kaskaskia, 164, 165-68; captures Vincennes, 168-71
Clark, William. *See* Lewis and Clark Expedition.
"Clermont," Robert Fulton's steamboat, 252-53
Clinch River, 137
Clinton, General, commands British in New York, 173
Clipper ships, 291, 292
Cloth-making on hand looms, 102 111, 124
Coach travel, in colonial days, 100, 105-6, 109, 114; of the Forty-Niners, 289, 295-97
Cody, William, Pony Express rider, 300-1
Colonial days, life in, 95 ff.
Colorado River, 230
Columbia River, 203
Columbus, Christopher, boyhood of, 3-5; education of, 5-6; interest of in finding a route to India and China, 6-7; is deceived by King John of Portugal, 7-9; is helped by Ferdinand and Isabella of Spain, 9 ff.; the voyage of, 11-12; discovers America, 12-13; in the New World, 13-15; returns to Spain, 16-17; last days of, 17-18
Columbus, Domenico, father of Christopher Columbus, 3 ff.
Communication. *See* Pony Express; Telegraph.

Index

Consitutional Convention, the, in Philadelphia, 176 ff.
Constitution of the United States, the, making of, 176 ff.
Continental Congress, First, meets in Philadelphia, 114-18; Second, meets in Philadelphia, 147 ff.
Cooper, Peter, builds the "Tom Thumb," 260 ff.
Cornwallis, General, in Virginia, 173-74; surrender of, 174-75
Costume
  Colonial, 106, 110, 114, 146, 147, 148, 149, 150, 151, 152, 168, 174, 177
  Colonial children, 98, 101, 110, 112-13, 183
  Dutch, 66-71, 98
  Elizabethan, 25, 27, 31, 33, 46, 48
  Indian, 14-15, 46, 48, 55, 58, 73, 78, 80, 98, 99, 201
  Pioneer, 122, 130, 131, 139, 140, 221, 222, 225
  Pirate, 207
  Puritan, 40, 53, 55, 56, 58
  Quaker, 75, 80
  Spanish, 15th and 16th centuries, 2, 5, 8, 10, 12, 14-15, 20
Cotton, planted by Oglethorpe, 89
Cotton gin, invention of, 245 ff.
Cotton industry, 244
Cotton mill, first in America, 241 ff.
Council Bluff, on Missouri River, 279
Covered wagon, the, 125, 216, 219, 220
Cradle, for reaping grain, 255, 256
"Croatoan," 32
Cumberland Gap, 137
Custis, Jack and Patsy, at Mount Vernon, 100 ff.

DARE, ANANIAS, and his wife, 30 ff.
Dare, Virginia, 30
"Dark and bloody ground," 137, 165

Deane, Silas, in France, 163
Declaration of Independence, written, 149-50; signed, 152-53
Delaware. See Rodney, Caesar.
Dickinson, Mrs., in the Alamo, 233
Diggs, Mr. and Mrs., entertain the Washingtons, 105-6
"Discovery," Henry Hudson's ship, 63 ff.
"Discovery," ship of Jamestown colonists, 41
Dishes, wooden, made by Indians, 99
Drake, Sir Francis, 29
Dress. See Costume
Dutch, the, settle in New Amsterdam, 65; life of, 65-67; character of, 67-69; trouble of with Indians, 69, 70; submit to English, 72; in Pennsylvania, 82
Dutch East India Company, 61-63
Dyes, made by Indians, 99

EDEN, Governor, of Maryland, 107
Electricity, Franklin's experiments with, 161
"Eliza," ship used by Forty-Niners 291
Elizabeth, Queen, 24, 26
Elliott, Annie, friend of Morse, 268
Episcopalians, at Continental Congress, 116
Erie Canal, 280

FAIRFAXES, the, of Virginia, 107
Falls of the Ohio, 166
Ferdinand, King, and Isabella, Queen, of Spain, 9 ff.; 16-17
Finley, John, 128, 132-33, 134
First Continental Congress. See Continental Congress.
First Thanksgiving, 58-59
Flat Boats, 195, 217, 218
Flats, the, home of Peter Schuyler near Albany, 95 ff.
Fleet Prison, 83 ff.

Index

Florida, discovery of, 19
"Flying Cloud," clipper ship, 291, 292
Food, of the Indians and first settlers, corn, game, and fish, 28-29, 46, 57, 58-59; of the pioneers, 123, 129-30, 142-43
Forts. See names of forts.
Fort Marion, 21-22
Fort Sutter, California, 283 ff.
Fort Walla Walla, 281
Forty-Niners, the, 288 ff.; 295-97
Fountain of Youth, 19 ff.
Fourth of July, the first, 153
Fox, George, Quaker preacher, 76
France, and the United States, 162-63. See also Lafayette
Franklin, Benjamin, boyhood of, 159-60; printing press of, 159; experiments of with electricity, 161; writings of, 162; signs Declaration of Independence, 152; in France, 162-63; dress of, 162; at Constitutional Convention, 176 ff.
Franklin, Missouri, 221, 225
Frémont, John C., the "Pathfinder," expedition of across the Rockies, 227 ff.
French and Indian War, 127-28
Frey, Johnnie, Pony Express rider, 297
Fulton, Robert, and the steamboat, 225, 250 ff.
Fur trade, 98-99, 124, 134 ff., 221 ff.

GALVESTON, Island, 231
Games, See Self-Testing Games
Gardens, colonial, 96, 101-2
Gates to the Rocky Mountains, 201
Genoa, Italy, home of Columbus, 3, 4, 18
George II, and Oglethorpe's colony, 86
Georgia, beginning of, 83 ff.
Germans, in Pennsylvania, 82
Gilbert, Sir Humphrey, 24

"Godspeed," ship of Jamestown colonists, 41
Gold, discovery of in California, 283 ff.; panning of, 286
Gold Diggings, the, 287, 293
Goodyear, Charles, and the rubber industry, 269 ff.
Gosnold, Captain, 41, 44
Grand Island, home of the Lafittes, 207 ff.
Greene, Mrs. Nathanael, encourages Eli Whitney to invent the cotton gin, 245 ff.
Grenville, Sir Richard, commander of Raleigh's expedition, 28; the silver cup of, 28-29
Grimes, John, defends the Lafittes, 208
Gulf of Mexico, 206, 230
Gumpf, Chris, friend of Morse, 250
Gunston Hall, home of the Masons, 100, 107

"HALF-MOON," Henry Hudson's ship, 60, 61, 63
Hamilton, Alexander, at the Constitutional Convention, 176 ff.; in charge of finances of the new nation, 190
Hamilton, General, at Detroit, 168-69; takes Vincennes, 169; yields to Clark, 171
Hancock, John, at Second Continental Congress, 147 ff.; signs Declaration of Independence, 152
Hays, Molly, See Molly Pitcher
Henderson, Judge Richard, employer of Boone, 137
Henry, Patrick, at First Continental Congress, 115 ff.; at Second Continental Congress, 147 ff.: governor of Virginia, 165, 166
History of the World, by Sir Walter Raleigh, 34
Home life, in the colonies, 58-59,

Index

Homes, on Roanoke Island, 30-31; at Jamestown, 44, 55-58; in New Amsterdam, 65-66; at Savannah, 87; Schuylers' "The Flats," 95 ff.; Mount Vernon, 100 ff.; pioneer, 129-33, 219-20; in Santa Fé, 223
Hotels. *See* Taverns
Houses. *See* Homes
Houston, Sam, defeats Mexicans in Texas, 236
Howland, John, 52
Hudson, Henry, looks for northern route to China, 60-61; explores Hudson River, 61-62; returns to Europe, 63; again looks for northern route to China, 63; icebound in Hudson Bay, 64; deserted by his men, 65; fate of unknown, 65
Hudson Bay, 65
Hudson River, 62, 65, 185, 252-53
Hunt, Robert, 45

ILLINOIS country, won by Clark, 171
India, trade with, 15
Indiana country, won by Clark, 171
Indians, American, found in New World, 13-14; in Florida, 20-21; on Roanoke Island, 28 ff., 32; around Jamestown, 45 ff.; in New England, 54 ff.; around New Amsterdam, 61 ff., 69 ff.; Penn's treaty with, 77-82; on the frontier, 127 ff., 165; west of the Mississippi, 196 ff., 296 ff.; of the Oregon country, 277-79
"India Rubber Man." *See* Goodyear, Charles
Inventions in America, 241 ff.; 243 ff.; 250 ff.; 254 ff.; 260 ff.; 264 ff.; 269 ff.
Irish, the, 26
Isabella, Queen. *See* Ferdinand, King of Spain 65-68, 95-98, 100-108, 109-12; on the frontier, 123-26, 129-33

JACKSON, ANDREW, accepts aid of the Lafittes in War of 1812, 210
Jackson, Dr. Charles Thomas, influences Morse, 265
James I., 32 ff., 41, 44
James River, 44, 46, 49
Jamestown, Virginia, 34, 41 ff., 44 ff., 87
Jefferson, Thomas, at Second Continental Congress, 149 ff.; writes Declaration of Independence, 149 ff.; signs Declaration of Independence, 152; in France, 163; influence of, 190; and the West, 195-96
Jefferson River, 201
John, King of Portugal, 7 ff.
"John Motley," schooner used by Austin's settlers, 231

KANSAS CITY, 282
Kaskaskia, fort of, captured by George Rogers Clark, 164 ff.
Kaskaskia River, 164, 165
Kentucky, 137 ff., 165, 166, 217, 230
Kentucky River, 139
King's College (now Columbia University), New York, 108
Knitting, in early days, 96, 102, 111, 112, 131

LAFAYETTE, in America, 172 ff.
Lafitte, Jean and Pierre, pirates, 206 ff.
Lane, Ralph, 28
Lee, Richard Henry, at First Constitutional Congress, 115 ff.; at Second Continental Congress, 147 ff.; signs Declaration of Independence, 152
Lewis, Meriwether. *See* Lewis and Clark Expedition
Lewis and Clark Expedition, 195 ff.; map of, 197; opens door to West, 205, 217

Index

Lexington, Virginia, home of Cyrus McCormick, 254, 257
Library, the, 35, 89, 118, 143, 178, 211, 236, 272, 302
"Lively," ship used by Austin's settlers, wrecked, 230
Loe, Thomas, Quaker preacher, 76
London Company, 41
London Plague (Great Plague of London, 1664-65), 75-76
Lost Colony, the, 29 ff.
Louisiana Purchase, 196
Lovejoy, General, 282
Loyalists, 149
Lumbering, in California, 283-84

McCORMICK, CYRUS, inventor of the reaper, 254 ff.
McCormick, Robert, father of Cyrus, 254 ff.
McDowell, Colonel James, neighbor of the McCormicks, 256
McKean, Thomas, delegate to Second Continental Congress, 150, 151
Madison, Dolly, 189
Madison, James, at the Constitutional Convention, 176 ff.; pardons the Lafittes, 211
Mail-wagon, travel by means of, 191 ff.
Mandan Indians, 199
Manteo, Indian friend of the English, 28
Marion, Francis, 156-57
Maryland breakfast, 106
Masons, the, of Virginia, 100, 107
Massachusetts, and the Revolution, 116
Massasoit, an Indian chief, 57
Massie, Captain William, neighbor of the McCormicks, 256
"Mayflower," ship of the Pilgrims, 51 ff.
Medicine, backwoods, 132
Mexico, rule of in Texas, 231-32
Mississippi River, 165, 171, 253
Missouri Intelligencer, 222

Missouri River, and the westward movement, 196 ff., 279, 296
Molly Pitcher, 154-55
Monroe, James, 189-90
Morristown, N. J., home of Alfred Vail, 266
Morse, Samuel F. B., inventor of the telegraph, 264 ff.
Mount Airy, home of the Calverts, 107, 108
Mount Vernon, life at, 100 ff.

NEGROES, in old New York, 97-98; in early Virginia, 102-3
Nelson, Governor, at Yorktown, 175
Nelson house, at Yorktown, 175
Nevada, 288
New Amsterdam, 65 ff., 72
New England, 49, 53
New Orleans, 206 ff., 230
Newport, Captain, 41, 43
New Year's Eve customs, 97-98
New York, social life in days of first president of U. S., 187; streets of in days of first president, 188-89. *See also* New Amsterdam
Nicolls, Colonel, 72
"Nina," ship of Columbus, 10, 12
Nixon, John, at Second Continental Congress, 152
North Carolina, home of the Boones, 126, 136
North Carolinians, in French and Indian War, 127

OGLETHORPE, JAMES, interested in English prisoners, 83 ff.; plans a colony in Georgia, 86; sails for Georgia with colony; 86-87; starts settlement at Savannah, 87; plans of for his colony, 87-89
Ohio country, 217
Ohio River, and the westward

310

Index

movement, 139, 165, 166, 171, 195, 217, 218, 253
Okee, Indian idol, 46
Old Silver Nails. *See* Stuyvesant, Peter
Omaha Indians, 197
Onas, Indian name of William Penn, 78
Oregon country, ownership of in dispute, 281
Oregon question, 282
Oregon Trail, the, opened, 277 ff., 288
Oxford College, 75, 83

PACIFIC TELEGRAPH, 302
Packet boat, comes to Mount Vernon, 103-4
Palos, Columbus sails from, 11; Columbus returns to, 16
Pawtucket, R. I., first mill at, 242-43
Peale, Angelica, 183 ff.
Peale, Charles Willson, 184
Peddlers, in colonial days, 132
Penn, Sir William, father of William Penn, 74, 75-76
Penn, William, childhood of, 74; education of, 75; becomes a Quaker, 76; in France and Ireland, 75-76; plans colony in America, 76; goes to Pennsylvania, 77; makes treaty with Indians, 77 ff.; lays out Philadelphia, 82
Penn's Woods, 73 ff. *See also* Pennsylvania
Pennsylvania, 77, 166, 242. *See also* Penn's Woods
Pennsylvania Dutch, 82
Pewter, used in colonial days, 96, 109, 129
Philadelphia, founded by William Penn, 74; naming of, 82; First Continental Congress at, 114 ff.; Second Continental Congress at, 147 ff.; entertains George Washington, 184 ff.; capital of U. S., 189

Pilgrims, sail for America, 51; the voyage of, 52-53; reach Cape Cod, 53; settle in Plymouth, 54; dealings of with the Indians, 54 ff.; celebrate the First Thanksgiving, 58-59
"Pinta," ship of Columbus, 10, 12
Pioneers, the, life of, 123 ff., 217 ff.; homes of, 219-20
Pittsburgh, on the route to the West, 166, 171
Plymouth, England, 24
Plymouth, New England, 54 ff., 87
Plymouth Company, 41
Plymouth Rock, 54
Pocahontas, 48-49
Pohick Church, 100
Polo, Marco, 6-7, 14
Ponce de León, discovers Florida, 19; attempts to settle Florida, 20-21; death of, 21
Pony Express, the, need for, 295-97; beginning of, 297; first trip of, 297-99; riders of, 297 ff.; stories of, 299-301; importance of, 302
Poor Richard's Almanack, by Benjamin Franklin, 162
Porto Rico, 19
Post office, of the Forty-Niners, 295-96
Potomac River, 104
Powhatan, Indian king, 47 ff.
Prairie schooners, 288. *See also* Covered Wagons
Printing press, Franklin's, 159
Puritans, at Continental Congress, 116

QUAKERS, in England, 75 ff.; and the Revolution, 116; at Continental Congress, 116, 117; the Boone family, 123 ff. *See also* Penn, William
Queen Anne, 95-96
"Quick-Silver Bob." *See* Morse, Samuel F. B.

Index

RAFTS, 217
Raleigh, Sir Walter, boyhood and early life of, 24-26; meets Queen Elizabeth, 26; gets her permission to plant a colony in the New World, 26-28; first expedition of, 27-28; second expedition of 28-29; lost colony of, 29 ff.; loses the Queen's favor, 32; thrown into Tower of London, 34; writes *History of the World*, 34; sails to South America, 34; imprisoned, 34; death of, 34
Raleigh Tavern, Williamsburg, Va., 116
Reaper, invention of, 254 ff.
Reed, General, of Pennsylvania, 154
Revolution. *See* American Revolution
Roads and highways, 109
Roanoke Island, 30-31
Rodney, Caesar, ride of, 150-52
Roff, Harry, 299
Rubber industry, 269 ff.
Rush, Dr. Benjamin, of Philadelphia, 115

SACAJAWEA, guide of Lewis and Clark Expedition, 199 ff.
Sacramento, Pony Express rider leaves, 299
Sacramento Valley, 283
St. Augustine, beginning of, 19, 21 ff.
St. Joseph, Mo., 297; Pony Express starts from, 297
St. Louis, 204, 225, 277, 279
Salmon, in Columbia River, 203
Salt-making, 141
Samoset, a friendly Indian, 55 ff.
Sampler, picture of, 94; made in colonial days, 96
San Marco. *See* Fort Marion
San Salvador, island on which Columbus first landed, 14

Santa Anna, General, besieges the Alamo, 233 ff.
Santa Fé, 222, 223, 224
Santa Fé Trail, 221
"Santa Maria," ship of Columbus, 10, 12
"Sarah Constant," ship of Jamestown colonists, 41
Savannah, founding of, 87 ff.
Schuyler, Catalina, 95 ff.
Schuyler, Peter, dealings of with the Indians, 95, 98-99
Schuyler barn, the, 96-97
Second Continental Congress. *See* Continental Congress
Self-Testing Games, 36, 90, 118, 143, 178, 212, 236, 272, 302
Shack-a-maxon, the Place of Kings, 77
Silk, in the New World, 88
Sioux Indians, 196
Slater, John, brother of Samuel, 243
Slater, John, nephew of Samuel, founder of Slater fund, 244
Slater, Mrs. Samuel, suggests making of cotton sewing thread, 244
Slater, Samuel, starts the first cotton mill in America, 241 ff.
Smith, Captain John, early adventures of, 42; fights with three Turks, 42-43; imprisoned on the way to Virginia, 43; trial and vindication of, 45; trades with Indians for corn, 46 ff.; explorations of, 47; captured by Powhatan, 47-48; saved by Pocahontas, 48-49; as president of the Council, 49; is badly burned in explosion, 49; returns to England, 49; later explorations of, 49, 53; estimate of, 49-50
Soap-making, 112, 285
Something to Do, 37, 91, 119, 144, 179, 213, 237, 273, 303
South Carolina, 87

Index

Spain, in the New World, 16 ff., 19 ff., 24, 28, 44, 87
Spalding, Dr. and Mrs., accompany Marcus Whitman to Oregon, 279 ff.
"Speedwell," ship of the Pilgrims, 51
Spinning, in colonial days, 102, 110, 131
Spinning wheel, 110
Squanto, a friendy Indian, 55 ff.
Stage-coach, 276. See also Coach travel
Standish, Captain Miles, 53, 54, 57
Steamboat, first in America. See "Clermont"
Steam engine, for railroads, 260 ff.
Stuyvesant, Peter, "Old Silver Nails," 68 ff.
"Sully," Morse's voyage on, 265
Sutter, Captain John, in California, 283 ff.
Swedes, in Pennsylvania, 82

TAMINENT, an Indian chief, 79 ff.
Taverns, in colonial days, 109, 115
Telegraph, invention of, 264 ff.
Tennessee, 217, 230
Tennessee River, 167
Testing Games. See Self-Testing Games
Texas, 217, 229 ff., 233 ff.
Thanksgiving Day. See First Thanksgiving
Thaxter, John, tutor of John Quincy Adams, 111, 113
"Tom Thumb," the races, with horse car, 260 ff.
Tories. See Loyalists
Tower Hill, London, 74
Tower of London, 34
Transportation. See Coach travel; Covered wagon; Flat-boat; Steamboat; Steam engine; Travel

Trappers, in the West, 221 ff.
Travel, in days of first president, 191 ff. See Transportation
Travis, General William B., defends the Alamo, 233 ff.
Trenton, N. J., celebrates Washington's triumphal progress to New York, 185
Turks' Heads, on Captain John Smith's shield, 42-43
Turnpike gate, 193
Twining, Thomas, travels of in America, 191 ff.
Tyler, President, and Oregon, 282

UNIVERSITY of the City of New York, 265
Utah, 288

VAIL, ALFRED, helps Samuel F. B. Morse, 266 ff.
Van Dyck, a Dutch settler, 69
Vincennes, captured by George Rogers Clark, 168 ff.
Virginia, Raleigh's attempts to colonize, 27 ff.; first permanent settlement in, 41 ff.; as a colony during the Revolution, 116 ff.

WABASH RIVER, 169-70
Walla Walla. See Fort Walla Walla
Wampum, 73-74, 99
Wanchese, Indian of Roanoke Island, 28
War of 1812, fighting in near New Orleans, 209-11
Warrior's path, 134
Washington, George, at Mount Vernon, 100 ff.; in French and Indian War, 127-28; at First Continental Congress, 114 ff.; at Second Continental Congress, chosen commander-in-chief, 147-48; takes command, 148; fights British in New York, 154; friend of Lafayettes,

Index

172-73; victory of at Yorktown, 175; bids farewell to his army, 176; at the Constitutional Convention, 176 ff.; chosen first president of the U. S., 178; portrait of, 182; on his way to the inauguration, 183 ff.; inauguration of in New York, 187, 188; as president in New York and Philadelphia, 187 ff.; described by Thomas Twining, 194

Washington, Lawrence, half-brother of George Washington, 103

Washington, Martha, 100 ff.; 187, 190, 194

Washington, D. C., laid out, 189; in days of first president, 194

Weaving, in colonial days, 110-11, 124

Webster, Daniel, 282

Weepers' Tower, 60, 61

"Welcome," ship of William Penn, 77

Westward movement, 217 ff.

"What Hath God Wrought," first telegraphic message, 268

White, Governor John, 28, 30 ff.

Whitman, Marcus, reads of western Indians, 277; determines to take the Bible to them, 279; goes to St. Louis, 279; goes to Oregon, 280 ff.; welcomed by Indians, 281; returns to Washington to beg the government to keep Oregon country, 281-82; wins consent, 282; leads band of settlers over Oregon Trail, 282

Whitney, Eli, inventor of the cotton gin, 245 ff.

Wilderness Road, 137, 219

William and Mary College, 149

Williamsburg, Va., 116

Windsor chairs, 103

Wingfield, Governor, 44-45

Wool, combing, 3, 6; spinning and weaving of, 102, 110

Wool industry, 244

YADKIN RIVER, 126
Yale College, 264
Yorktown, Va. 175

www.ingramcontent.com/pod-product-compliance
Lightning Source LLC
Chambersburg PA
CBHW021354290426
44108CB00010B/231